A CONCISE GUIDE

to Understanding Music

by Graham Wade

1 2 3 4 5 6 7 8 9 0

Visit us on the Web at www.melbay.com — E-mail us at email@melbay.com

Graham Wade, General Editor of the Mel Bay 'All About Music' Series, is Tutor in Classic Guitar for the Universities of Leeds and York and was formerly Head of Strings at the Leeds College of Music, England. A contributor for *The New Grove Dictionary of Music and Musicians,* he has written for various periodicals including *Soundboard, Guitar Review, Classical Guitar, Guitar International, Il Fronimo, The Strad, Musical Times, The Times,* etc. His previous books include: *A Concise History of the Classic Guitar, A New Look at Segovia, His Life, His Music, Vols 1 & 2* (with Gerard Garno), *Segovia-A Celebration of the Man and His Music, Maestro Segovia, Traditions of the Classical Guitar, Joaquín Rodrigo-Concierto de Aranjuez, Distant Sarabandes-The Solo Guitar Music of Joaquín Rodrigo, A Guitarist's Guide to Bach,* and *Gina Bachauer-A Pianist's Odyssey.*

CONTENTS

List of Illustrations 5

Foreword 6

PART I – THE BASIC ESSENTIALS

1. The Composer 7
2. Sound 10
3. The Musical Scale 14
4. Plainsong and the Modes 18
5. The Development of Scales and Tonality 20
6. Melody 25
7. Counterpoint 26
8. Harmony 28

PART II – INSTRUMENTS - NOTATION

9. The Instruments of Music 29
10. Notation 32
11. The Revival of Improvisation 35
12. Reading Musical Notation 36

PART III – MUSICAL FORM

13. Musical Form 38
14. Expectations of Musical Form 41
15. Binary and Ternary 43

PART IV – MUSIC FOR A PURPOSE

16. Sacred Music 46
17. Music and Words 51
18. Music and Movement 54

PART V – MUSICAL EXPLORATIONS

19. The Suite 58
20. Rondeau, Rondo 63
21. Theme and Variations 65
22. Earlier Forms of Variations 68
23. The Art of Fugue 70
24. The Mechanisms of Fugue 71
25. Sonata 74
26. The Classical Era 78
27. Sonata Form 81
28. The Symphony Orchestra in the Concert Hall 84
29. The Development of the Symphony 86
30. The Symphonies of Haydn 88

31. The Symphonies of Mozart and Beethoven 89
32. The Continuation of Symphony 92
33. Concerto 94
34. The Form of the Concerto 97
35. The Operas of Mozart and Beethoven 101

PART VI – THE 19TH CENTURY
36. Early 19th Century Romanticism 103
37. Schumann, Chopin and Liszt 105
38. Hector Berlioz 109
39. Opera in the 19th Century 111
40. Johannes Brahms 116
41. The Music of Nationalism 117

PART VII – THE 20TH CENTURY
42. The Age of Change 120
43. Claude Debussy 123
44. Maurice Ravel 125
45. Erik Satie 127
46. Serialism 128
47. Spanish Music 133
48. Heitor Villa-Lobos 136
49. Through Folk Songs to the 20th Century 137
50. The Genius of Stravinsky 139
51. Composers and Dictators 141
52. Charles Ives 143
53. Edgard Varèse 145
54. George Gershwin 146
55. Aaron Copland and Samuel Barber 147
56. Developments in Italy 150
57. Olivier Messiaen 152
58. John Cage 155
59. British Composers 158
60. Witold Lutoslawski 160
61. Leonard Bernstein 162
62. The Fulfillment of the 20th Century 163
63. Pierre Boulez 165
64. György Ligeti 168
65. Karlheinz Stockhausen 169
66. Minimalism 171
67. The 21st Century 172

LIST OF ILLUSTRATIONS

1. Ludwig van Beethoven - the great composer 7
2. Spanish flamenco guitarists improvise their music 8
3. Minstrels at a Banquet by M. Wohlgemuth (engraving of 1491) 12
4. A new design of guitar for the 21st century 13
5. Monks singing (from a Venetian engraving, 1512) 18
6. The sitar, played by Lila Pancholi 30
7. Early notation from the 13th century 32
8. An avant-garde score - Bussotti's Siciliano 33
9. The Church of St Thomas, Leipzig, where J.S. Bach was Cantor 46
10. Elgar depicted conducting an oratorio in 1904 48
11. A portrait of Claudio Monteverdi 52
12. A scene from Handel's opera Flavio (1723) 54
13. The ballet in a 19th century engraving 55
14. 16th century dancers 56
15. An edition of the lute works of J.S. Bach 58
16. A round dance in northern Spain, early 20th century 63
17. A biography of Domenico Scarlatti 75
18. A portrait of C.P.E. Bach 77
19. A book about Haydn first published in 1902 79
20. A symphony orchestra performs at the Royal Albert Hall, London 84
21. Woman playing a viol (Tobias Stimmer, c. 1570) 87
22. A portrait of Mozart on one of the many books about his life 90
23. A book on Beethoven by William Kinderman 91
24. An 18th century orchestra, ideal for performing concertos 95
25. The Greek pianist, Gina Bachauer, performing a concerto 96
26. A scene in the harem from *The Seraglio* by Mozart 101
27. A biography of Robert Schumann 105
28. A portrait of Chopin by Delacroix on a Chopin biography 106
29. Liszt at the piano 107
30. An early lithograph portrait of Hector Berlioz 110
31. An early portrait of Rossini 112
32. Richard Wagner in characteristic pose 113
33. A satirical caricature of Verdi 114
34. A biography of Brahms 116
35. A recording of Tchaikovsky's symphonies 117
36. The 20th century image of the rock musician 122
37. Claude Debussy 124
38. The collected writings of Maurice Ravel 126

39. Erik Satie, as portrayed by Picasso 127
40. Arnold Schoenberg 130
41. Manuel de Falla 134
42. Heitor Villa-Lobos conducting 136
43. A short biography of Béla Bartók 138
44. Stravinsky featured in the Master Musicians series 140
45. Charles Ives depicted on a recording of his Symphonies Nos 2 & 3 143
46. George Gershwin at the keyboard 146
47. A biography of Aaron Copland 148
48. A recording of Samuel Barber's music 149
49. Conversations with Olivier Messiaen 153
50. John Cage's writings 157
51. A biographical study of Benjamin Britten 159
52. A musical study of Witold Lutoslawski 160
53. A recording of Leonard Bernstein's Chichester Psalms 162
54. The collected writings of Pierre Boulez 166
55. A biography of György Ligeti 168
56. Karlheinz Stockhausen 170

Foreword

This book, intended for all who wish to understand more about music, looks at the basic elements of one of humanity's greatest means of artistic expression. Beginning with 'the composer' (that mysterious presence who provides whatever music we listen to), we move to developments over the course of history and the amazing progress of music during the 20th century.

Music constantly changes. One fashion yields to another, certain styles or instruments become neglected and are less popular than before, new structures and new sounds emerge all the time. It can all be rather confusing. Yet the adventure of music, past and present, is there for us to explore and enjoy, a life-long journey of discovery.

I would like to thank William Bay and all his staff at Mel Bay Publications Inc. for making this book and this series possible. I must also thank my wife, Elizabeth, for her invaluable editorial assistance.

Graham Wade
General Editor, *ALL ABOUT MUSIC SERIES*
February, 2003

PART I
THE BASIC ESSENTIALS

1. The Composer

All music has to begin somewhere and it originates, one way or another, with a 'composer'. A composer is a craftsman, a maker, a builder, also a designer, bringing into the world something which did not previously exist and which may prove of great value to humanity. A carpenter uses wood to build his creations and an architect moulds concrete, stone, steel and other materials into useful habitable structures. The composer works with the invisible but powerful possibilities of sound, filling the world with patterns, vibrations and musical shapes.

Ludwig van Beethoven - the great composer

The composer feels a need to create music, often being driven by an inner compulsion from a very early age to write pieces. But, as well as creating music and performing on various instruments, composers must also listen to the music going on around them, observing and absorbing techniques and styles.

Every nation, race, tribe, creed and social background produces people skilled in the art of music. In many cultures music is rarely written down formally, but traditions and techniques are passed from one generation to another orally. Improvisation is vital here and the roles of composer and player are virtually one and the same.

However, improvisation is rarely a matter of playing whatever comes into one's head. It usually involves a rather complicated set of guidelines within which the music functions. The player/composer must first master these rules before being in a position to advance the art according to his or her own personal insights.

Spanish flamenco guitarists improvise their music

Indian music with its intricate ragas, Andalusian flamenco with numerous forms and variations, and most styles of jazz improvisation with fixed chord sequences derived from melodies, are examples of structured, informed improvisation. Many varieties of African, Arabic and Oriental folk music also operate along similar lines. Composers in these cultures submit themselves to a rigid discipline in order to master playing and compositional techniques. Such apprenticeships are often lifelong as well as being extremely demanding, both physically and mentally.

In European music over the last five centuries improvisation for soloists and groups has frequently been a necessary part of a musician's life. But the art of composing became more and more closely linked with writing music down using a device now called musical notation. Notation enables composers to reach a wide international public of players and listeners, and to pass on to later generations the essence of their musical ideas.

One practical result of notation was to burden the composer with a great task. Literally millions of notes have to be put down on paper one way or another. Until the invention of the computer in recent decades, the composer had no mechanical means to lighten the labor. A piece of music of five minutes playing time, composed for a large orchestra, might take the composer hundreds of hours to write down. As well as writing the notes down, the composer must add suitable expression marks conveying many subtle distinctions of meaning.

The preparation of orchestral parts was (and still is) a massive undertaking. The composer must not only be an imaginative musician, but also a patient worker, willing to put up with long periods of comparative drudgery in order to achieve something of value. It cannot be wondered at if some composers in history seem to have pursued a rather isolated existence as they struggled with their sonatas, symphonies, concertos and operas, slowly shaping them in their heads and putting notes down on paper.

Of course, for the listener all composers from all cultures deal with the same basic materials. They create melodies and provide accompaniments, they set our feet tapping or our heads swaying with rhythmic patterns, they borrow or imitate sounds from the world of nature and humanity.

Great melodies come from the properties of the human voice and almost all musical instruments relate to the voice. The most exciting rhythms are taken in the first instance from the universal beating of heart and pulse, and from the complex varied activities of the body in dancing, movement and gesture. Natural sounds such as the sea, trees, streams, birdsong, galloping horses and thunderstorms can provide inspiration for composers. But so also can the noise of human activity such as the movements of men pulling on ropes at sea, the clatter of the spinning wheel, the rhythms of machines, the blacksmith's hammer or the marching of armies.

Just as the painter makes us more aware of color, form and movement in the visual world, so the composer has the capacity to make us more sensitive to the world of hearing. The story of music tells how musicians strive constantly to create patterns of sound.

2. Sound

Sound is vibration. From birth onwards we are absorbed, soothed, frightened, or indifferent to, millions of varieties of vibration. It just happens that we have been born into the noisiest period of history ever experienced, a fact people who live in cities come to terms with. In the skies above, in streets, in factories, even in offices, there is usually noise, noise, and more noise - aircraft, pneumatic drills, automobiles and trucks, bulldozers, trains, etc.!

Music has to take full account of the times we live in. Contemporary music often reflects the turmoil and cacophony of daily living and composers have been keen to develop novel techniques for creating a wide array of sound effects. Electronic music, ingenious uses of amplification, and numerous evolving species of electric instruments (including keyboard, basses and violins, as well as guitars) have changed the textures of musical sound. It is not surprising if new instruments are invented for composers to exploit. Musical tastes are in a perpetual state of change throughout all historical eras. The actual make-up of ensembles and orchestras from the Middle Ages onwards never remains static or rigidly fixed.

Musical development is stabilized by various factors. For one thing the human ear predetermines the range and intensity of sound available to the composer. Sounds which are too high-pitched (such as the notes at the top end of the pianoforte) are not really convenient for sustained composition being both monotonous and indistinguishable from each other to the average human ear. Similarly, sounds which are too soft or too loud are not acceptable over a long period, though they may be tolerable for a little while. (Prolonged exposure to sounds of great volume can, of course, damage the sensitive mechanism of the ear.)

'Minstrels at a Banquet' by M. Wohlgemuth (engraving of 1491)

Unfamiliar instruments have always been welcomed by composers and new combinations of existing and accepted instruments are a common feature of the development of orchestral and group music. Nowadays, composers experiment similarly with electronic feedback, multiple tape recorders and many kinds of synthesizer, and guitar makers experiment with new shapes of familiar older instruments.

A new design of guitar for the 21st century

Another constant factor in the process of composition is the capability
of the human voice. Music tends to be written for the more comfortable ranges
of the various types of voice, generally avoiding too much concentration on
extremes of sound at either end of 'high' and 'low'. In this instance too many
low notes and too many high notes are not only potentially tedious for the
listener but can also strain the singer's voice. The composer has to learn to
respect the possibilities and limitations of the human vocal cords.

Each kind of voice, ranging from the deep bass to the high soprano, possesses its own characteristic sound qualities. By mixing together several types of voice within a choir, composers through the ages have succeeded in creating amazingly varied patterns of vocal music. From the skilful combination of distinctive voices emerged those contrasting lines of sound known as 'counterpoint' and from this, after a due process of historical development, came the complexities of harmony.

The human voice was, after all, the original musical instrument and it remains the most evocative and compelling of all.

3. The Musical Scale

Anyone who has learned a musical instrument knows that those aspiring to become expert performers usually spend quite a lot of time practicing scales. Most professional musicians keep their playing muscles supple by daily exercises of this kind while singers find scales invaluable in developing the full range of the voice.

All this hard work is inspired by the knowledge that melody, harmony and musical theory are firmly based on the patterns of tones and half tones which form the foundation of European scales. The actual notes of the scales give us the raw materials of music from which composers can build their works.

The European scales took hundreds of years to develop to the system we are familiar with today. Other musical cultures, such as those of India, Arabia and the Far East, evolved totally different scale formations.

The word **scale** is derived from the Latin word *scala*, meaning a 'ladder'. By means of this ladder, music ascends or descends by a convenient sequence of rungs. In the Western scales each ladder is made up of eight principal steps. Each step is given a letter name, and the scale is named according to the letter it starts on. Here are the eight steps of the scale of C as seen on a keyboard:

As the scale is made up of eight notes, the distance or interval between the two C's is known as an **octave**, from the Latin word, *octo,* for 'eight'. The interval of the octave (notes which have the same letter name eight notes higher or lower), the essential boundary of all scales, is used by musicians the world over whatever their cultural environment. Stringed instruments, particularly those such as the violin, guitar, sitar, Arabian lute, etc. in which the player's left hand shortens the vibrating string length by pressing the string down onto the neck of the instrument, are all able to demonstrate that fact of physics which creates the octave.

If, for example, a violinist or guitarist, presses a string with the left hand onto the neck of the instrument at exactly the halfway mark between the two fixed points of the vibrating string, the player produces a note an octave higher than the open string itself. If the string is tuned to vibrate at a frequency of 440 times per second (which produces the note A), the octave note would vibrate at precisely double the frequency of the open string, i.e. at 880 vibrations per second. This simple fact of physics, that a vibrating string if divided into two equal parts will sound the same note an octave higher is the starting point for the construction of the scale.

Though all musical cultures throughout the world acknowledge the interval of the octave, few of them have come to the same conclusions on how the octave should be divided. If you examine a modern pianoforte keyboard with its black and white notes you can see how after centuries of theoretical discussion, the European ear decided to divide the octave. Each octave is divided into twelve equal parts, called **half tones** or **semitones**. By combining half tones and tones (a tone being two semitones) in a specific order of eight steps, the western major and minor scales are built up.

The West may have settled down to dividing the octave into twelve semitones, but it is possible for the human ear to distinguish not only semitones but also those notes which can exist in between the semitones, sometimes entitled **microtones**. In the musical traditions of other cultures the octave is indeed subdivided into these microtones. Thus the structure and shape of such scales sound very different from those favored by European composers.

In Indian music, as in the Western scale, the seven main notes plus one to make up the octave are used, but the octave itself is divided into no fewer than twenty-two *shrutis*. These are like the Western sharps and flats, though in this case being considered as not only sharp and flat but as 'extremely flat' and 'extremely sharp'. Arabic music is founded on a series of modes (to be dealt with later), and again the octave is subdivided far more than in Western music. The theory on which Arabic music is based goes back to the early Middle Ages.

From the characteristic patterns of scales within each musical culture, the nature of its melody is derived. Many varieties of scales have evolved through the centuries. Each part of the world grows accustomed to the characteristics of its own scales, and also to its own rhythms and instrumental textures.

To the Western ear the shifting tones and microtones of Indian, Arabic and Oriental music may, at first, sound disturbingly unfamiliar. Hearing music from a foreign culture can be like watching baseball or a game of poker and not knowing the rules. However, in recent years many people have become interested in listening to and learning about music from other cultures. This has resulted in a wider appreciation of the common ground between music of all five continents as well as in a useful understanding of essential differences.

4. Plainsong and the Modes

All of us at some time or other have heard the chanting of monks, even if only as part of a film or television documentary. Monastic chanting is a very distinctive type of singing and its origins go far back into early Christian history.

Such music is called **plainsong** (or *cantus planus* in Latin) and became formally established as appropriate music for divine worship by Pope Gregory I at the end of the 6th century. The music is also known as **Gregorian Chant** in his honor. This style was found to be very suitable for the communal singing of psalms and prayers.

Monks singing (from a Venetian engraving, 1512)

At certain times in history, the medieval authorities were anxious that music should not be too exciting or sensuous in divine service, and for this reason choral singing in parts and instrumental accompaniments were not always allowed. The music was kept as simple as possible in contrast to the vivid splendor of much sacred music of later centuries.

Gregorian chant achieves its particular sound and mood from the kind of scales the monks used. These scales, known as **modes,** were the direct ancestors of our modern Western scales, both major and minor. Music as we know it today is overwhelmingly indebted to those hundreds of years of tradition when the modes dominated musical composition.

The theory governing the construction of the modes once again concerns the division of the octave into suitably spaced tones and semitones. For all practical purposes eight modes were used, each mode containing its own characteristic qualities.

If we pick out a tune on a modern piano and use just the white notes, and none of the black notes, the music will sound modal. Each of the modes was eventually given a Greek name in order to distinguish it from the others. From the system of the modes our modern scales developed.

The **Ionian mode,** for example, follows the exact pattern of the scale of C major (shown on page 15). In the Ionian mode or C major scale the principal note of C seems to be emphasized sufficiently and composers were content to use this scale formation more and more.

Also of great significance was the **Aeolian mode,** which can be played on a keyboard by using the white notes A-B-C-D-E-F-G-A. This mode closely resembles the modern harmonic minor scale of A minor, which differs from the Aeolian mode by only one note (i.e. when the black note on the keyboard to the right of G, known as G sharp, is included, instead of the white note, G). In the 16th century composers began to prefer the sound of the note G sharp (rather than G), when they wrote compositions based on the Aeolian mode.

One reason for this may have been that to move from G sharp to A emphasizes the principal note of the scale more definitely and unmistakably. Thus, in this instance, a mode was slightly altered by the composers with the result that the new emerging scale was ultimately preferred and the old Aeolian mode became obsolete and dropped out of use.

5. The Development of Scales and Tonality

The modes influenced the composition of music from about 400 AD to the beginning of the 17th century. But composers became increasingly attracted to the ideas of **tonality,** and this meant the displacement of modal music. The modes themselves in either plainsong or instrumental compositions have the effect of weakening and diluting tonality. This means that each note of the modal scale is very much an equal partner. In a truly modal work you could finish on any note and it would sound like a reasonably final and complete ending.

But the modern Western scales of major and minor can only finish on the principal note of the scale, known as the **tonic** or **keynote**, i.e. that note on which the scale starts, opening the door of the scale and closing it firmly at the end of the composition. Tonality implies music which contains a particular significant 'tone' or note, to which the music consistently relates. 'Tonality' is not easily definable but fundamentally it means that a composer refers constantly to the tonic or keynote. The properties associated with that key or scale are assumed to be the central point, the home ground of the composition. It is possible to move away from the home ground, of course, and sometimes quite a long way, but sooner or later the central point will be returned to.

Steadily, the major and minor scales invaded the vocabulary of composers. For over three hundred years from 1600, music in Europe is really about tonality, the sense of relationships between sounds. Even nowadays when so many composers write music which is **atonal** (without a key), the majority of popular music is still deeply rooted in tonality. Everyday music such as national anthems, hymns, jingles, songs from the musicals, and most rock hits, all conclude in the home key.

The complexities of tonality are considerable. Looked at on paper the possibilities exploited by great composers are endless, yet, when the music in question is listened to, a supreme naturalness dominates the proceedings. More often than not the semi-miraculous jugglings of harmony, key, melodic movement, etc., as the composer shifts his music from the home ground to new country and back again, are accepted by the listener with satisfaction and pleasure. The effect is that desired by all art, of variety within unity.

Tonality begins (and ends) with a consideration of the scale. As we have seen, each scale consists of eight notes including the octave, and here we can take another look at the C major scale. This time the notes of the scale have been given the numbers 1 to 8 in Roman numerals, a form of identification known as the 'degrees of the scale'.

I   II   III   IV   V   VI   VII   VIII

Each degree of the scale has a name:

I Tonic

    II Supertonic

        III Mediant

            IV Subdominant

                V Dominant

                    VI Submediant

                        VII Leading note

                            VIII Tonic

Every note of the scale has its own influence and significance, just like the pieces on a chess board, some being more powerful in terms of tonality and sense of key than the others, depending on context. The relative importance of the notes of the scale, simply summarized, is as follows:

The first note of the scale, the **tonic** or **keynote**, is the king of the scale. Everything in tonality relates to the tonic in one way or another.

The next most powerful note in the scale is the fifth note from the tonic - the **dominant**. A chord founded on this note, or even the note itself, may herald the imminent return of king tonic.

The fourth note of the scale, the **subdominant**, also possesses some of this power returning us, as it were, to an awareness of the tonic.

The seventh note of the scale, the **leading note**, frequently leads us to the tonic itself.

The third note of the scale, the **mediant** (as it is halfway between the tonic and the dominant), has a special importance, for this note can tell us if the key is major or minor.

The sixth note, the **submediant**, is positioned a third below the tonic.

The second note is entitled the **supertonic**, being one above the tonic.

Tonality does not mean that a piece of music is just in one key throughout. The composer has the option to **modulate** into other keys. Far from weakening the home ground, **modulation** may well reinforce the tonality, just as absence from home in foreign lands may instil a longing for one's native country.

Moreover, each major key possesses a **relative minor**, just as conversely each minor key has a **relative major**. This family relationship between major and minor is an invaluable aid to a composer who wishes temporarily to change the mood of a particular piece without departing too far distant from the home key.

The mechanisms of modulation are in themselves quite complicated, but to the listener a satisfactory modulation can be a sudden sparkle of sun on a grey sea or a vision of a new world. In the hands of a master, modulation can be so subtle that one hardly realizes it is happening. Controlling a smooth transition from one key to another (and back again) is a necessary skill for the composer and corresponds to the expertise of a racing driver in changing gears around the circuit.

The use of tonality has frequently been compared to an artist's use of color in a painting. Many pictures are made up from one overall color scheme, with a few tints dominating the entire canvas. In such a design blue might have a closer relationship to green and yellow than it would to, say, bright red. To the sensitive ear musical keys interact one against another just as colors juxtaposed on a canvas can affect the discerning eye.

The subtle mixture of musical light and shade through tonality is not only a fascinating study, it is also the cornerstone of traditional Western music. Without at least a reasonable awareness of its implications and effects, the work of most composers is robbed of meaning.

6. Melody

The history of music, as one might expect, is about increasing levels of complexity. Choirs and orchestras get bigger, more and more types of instruments are invented and used, musical works in themselves become longer and more substantial, the art of musical notation becomes ever more intricate, and the performance of music on public occasions (such as concerts or operas) grows more expensive and more elaborate.

Gregorian chant could be performed by a few monks; an opera nowadays requires dozens of singers and musicians, many stagehands and a huge theater to achieve its effect. Yet all this development is rooted in the very nature of music itself. From the acorn of melody grows the mighty tradition of counterpoint and harmony, the musical oak tree which spans centuries.

The simplest musical texture (apart from just banging a drum or playing a single note on an instrument) is surely that of a solo voice singing a straightforward tune. To some extent the discovery of the voice's ability to pitch notes in a satisfying sequence is presumably how music began. Not many notes are needed to construct a little melody.

Some primitive cultures use only three or four notes in a song, these being subjected to both repetition (with its curiously hypnotic effect) and rhythmic variation. This leads to the performance of the same notes on a musical instrument such as bamboo pipes or a stringed gourd. Another sound is thus added to the musical vocabulary of the tribe. The tune itself can be accompanied by percussion to give a little density to the sound.

It was realized fairly early on in history how the chanting of melodies could be given body and form by sheer weight of numbers. Singing in a choir was discovered to be pleasurable for the participants and moving for the listeners. Choral singing took a central place in religious, political and social occasions, as it still does. To the resonances of vocal ensemble, could then be added percussion, pipes, lyres, etc. to provide variety.

Music was used on many occasions. Religious ceremonies (including weddings and funerals), civic occasions, marching songs for armies, work songs of many kinds, festive gatherings, the sung recitation of epic tales of love, bravery and great national events—these were contexts which music could celebrate or enhance. In all such communal music the art of melody rules supreme.

Throughout the world today music still elevates melody to a supreme position. In European folk song, in Oriental, Arabic and Indian music, the voice and its melodic weavings are a most important aspect. The instruments that have evolved (apart from percussion) recreate, in a subtle form, the basic patterns of sound borrowed from the singer.

7. Counterpoint

In the Middle Ages Western music developed an interest in the skills of **counterpoint** and **polyphony**. (Counterpoint: Latin - *contrapunctus* from *contra punctum* meaning 'against note'.) Ever since, musicians in the West have been fascinated by the musical effects which occur when against a single melody sung by one person, another melody is voiced at the same time. And why not go further and sing three, four, or half a dozen melodies simultaneously? Thus began the **contrapuntal** tradition, contrapuntal being the adjective derived from counterpoint.

Polyphony ('many-voiced') is the ideal word to describe the choral music of several centuries. Each section of the choir pursues an independent line of melody, yet however many parts are included, each fits into the grand design with the neat precision of a Swiss clock. (The same principles of composition then became characteristic of instrumental music as well.)

Polyphony still flourishes in the realm of ecclesiastical music. The great cathedrals of the world and their choirs continue the tradition of previous ages and the masterpieces brought into being by the geniuses of counterpoint, such as Palestrina and J. S. Bach, enthral modern music lovers.

8. Harmony

Developing from counterpoint came a new interest in the mysteries of **harmony**. Composers became more and more intrigued by the chemistry of sound, by what happens when one musical ingredient is added to another.

During the 17th and 18th centuries, the independent voices and instruments favored by contrapuntal styles tended towards a more unified method of composing music. Counterpoint and harmony became established as equal partners in the study of music. Previously the art of music had consisted primarily of the subtle weaving together of individual threads of sound. Now composers became absorbed in harmonic blocks of sound, thinking about music not in horizontal or linear terms, but in vertical lines of progressive chordal sequences.

The second half of the 18th century established beyond doubt which way Western music was to go. By then contrapuntal traditions were beginning to sound a little old-fashioned, and different ideas about how music should be composed were becoming firmly rooted.

It was a momentous period in the development of musical history. From then on until the 20th century it was harmony, not counterpoint, which dominated the principles of western music.

PART II
INSTRUMENTS - NOTATION

9. The Instruments of Music

The variety of instruments is infinite, yet the actual means by which musical instruments can be made to sound are limited to basic methods: plucking or bowing a string, blowing, drumming or knocking.

Musicologists have grouped the various types of instruments into the following four families. These are:

Idiophones: for knocking, including cymbals, triangle or bells, or instruments such as xylophones or glockenspiels.

Membranophones: the drum family, in which a membrane or skin is stretched across a resonating cavity.

Chordophones: all stringed instruments, whether plucked (like the harp) or bowed (like the cello).

Aerophones: for blowing, such as trumpets, clarinets, flutes, bagpipes, whistles, etc.

These four groups are useful for general reference but the excitement now begins. The sheer range and scope of different types of instruments means that each culture tends to specialize in its own characteristic sounds. Chordophones of the plucked variety, for example, will include instruments as different as the Indian sitar, the Spanish guitar, the Arabic lute and the Russian balalaika.

The sitar - played here by Lila Pancholi (Northamptonshire Newspapers Ltd)

Aerophones range from the Jewish shofar (ram's horn) to the giant Alpine horn, and include the pipes of Pan, the harmonica and the trombone.

Musical instruments are known for their power to evoke the culture of particular countries. The Japanese koto, the Appalachian banjo, the Australian Aboriginal didgeridoo and the Scottish bagpipes instantly conjure up an image of their homelands. A few notes played on one of these is sufficient to create the sense of 'being there'. This strong identity of national music is mainly brought about by instrumental color.

These colors can also recall bygone historical eras. The sound of lutes and viols will bring to life the court of Elizabeth I or can be used effectively for staging a play by Shakespeare. Crumhorns, recorders, sackbuts and citterns in 'early music' are characteristic of the Middle Ages, whilst the tinkling of the harpsichord is forever reminiscent of the Baroque style of music. Similarly the massive sounds of a huge orchestra are associated with the 19th century expansion of instrumental textures across a large musical canvas.

Instrumentation is a vital quality in all music. The listener learns to distinguish between various instruments and to link certain sounds with specific periods of musical development. Style, scope and length in musical composition are closely related to instrumental color. A symphony written for a hundred-piece orchestra would be disappointing if it lasted for only five minutes. We expect something more substantial from such a large body of musicians. On the other hand, a suite written for harpsichord or small ensemble might be tedious if prolonged for more than about a quarter of an hour.

The umbilical relationship between the shape, form and structure of compositions and the instruments available to the composer at any given time should not be forgotten. In this instance the message is indeed the medium. Though accepted conventions may be transcended by genius at all times throughout musical history, an instrument (or a particular group of instruments) will to a large extent limit the composer's imagination in one way or another. The composer's ability to get the best out of available instrumental resources in unprecedented ways is one of the main aspects of musical development.

10. Notation

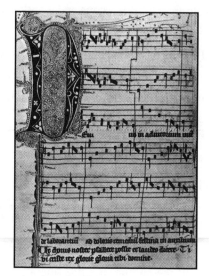

Early notation from the 13th century (Royal Library, Turin)

It took hundreds of years for musical notation to become as reliable and satisfactory as it is today. Composers now possess an international language of music through which they are able to communicate to a wide public. Various symbols, signs and marks have been evolved to give the performer a lot of information in a remarkably small space. Pitch, duration, and rhythm of individual notes, as well as phrasing, volume, speed, shading and other subtleties, can all be conveyed through notation. A composer has the opportunity to make clear his musical thoughts through a tried and tested method whether writing for a child learning the recorder or for a large professional orchestra.

The system of writing down music is still not considered to be absolutely perfect and composers continue to create their own radical innovations, as in this example:

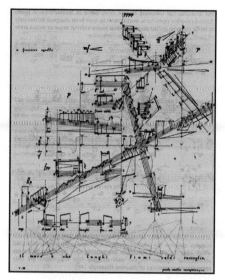

An avant-garde score - Bussotti's Siciliano
(Courtesy of Edizioni Bèrben)

Some instrumental techniques and sounds (especially in contemporary music) are extremely difficult to indicate on paper. The above example was intended for twelve male voices. Each singer follows any part of the score he cares to choose, performing the line at any speed and any register, to produce music which is 'chaotic and uncontrollable'. Such notation is not immediately comprehensible to most musicians and would need a page or two of instructions from the composer.

Music of the past also poses problems of reading and correct interpretation. Obscurities of various kinds abound in manuscripts of earlier centuries. The actual signs and indications may remain the same but over the years the meaning of these can alter, with the result that musicologists spend a great deal of time trying to establish just exactly how those early composers intended their music to sound.

In recent decades the Early Music Movement, encouraging research into authentic instruments and performance techniques through the ages, has revolutionized concepts of understanding and playing music from the distant past.

(Following the invention of recording technology it also became possible, for the first time in cultural history, to listen to performances of music by previous generations and to analyze many vital differences in their approach from performing practices of the present day. It became clear that even late 19th century and early 20th century interpretations of Western musical masterpieces were significantly different from later developments.)

The effects on Western music of the steady advances in the techniques of notation have been profound. As a result of being able to write down their music, composers have been free to indulge their imaginations. Restrictions imposed by length, number and ability of performers, and types of instruments available can be ignored. Notation allows ambitious projects to be undertaken at the composer's leisure. Even if a composer's work is not performed in his lifetime, it can be preserved for posterity. Later generations may ultimately recognize the merit of a composition that has long languished in neglect.

Composers such as Bach, Mozart, Beethoven, Chopin, and Liszt were considered to be among the finest virtuoso instrumentalists of their day. They wrote down their works both for personal performance and for publication and consequently their brilliant compositions still challenge the minds and abilities of the world's great players.

Beethoven, one of the outstanding pianists of his time (before deafness forced him to retire from public performance) composed his greatest works for piano, string quartet and orchestra, long after he became physically incapable of hearing the notes. The existence of a valid system of writing music down enabled him to make full use of his imaginative powers as a composer. We tend to take for granted the marvellous convenience of notation, but without it, the glories of European music could never have been achieved and perpetuated.

11. The Revival of Improvisation

It could be argued that though notation liberates the composer it may, in contrast, have the effect of shackling the poor performer, who has to submit to the composer's will as revealed on the page. The player's sole function, it seems, is to recreate notes put down by somebody else with no scope for his own individuality or creative musical gifts.

This was not always so. Between the 16th and 19th centuries, the player was expected to be able to embellish and improvise on the composer's written guidelines. In our own century composers have tried to restore some of this initiative to the player by including in the score moments of improvisation when the performer's musical contribution can be added to the composer's.

This recalls an important feature of the 18th century concerto, known as the **cadenza**, when a performer playing with the orchestra was expected to introduce a brief solo section into the work either actually improvised on the spot or composed by himself before the concert. In this way a balance could be achieved between the demands of the composer and the performer's personal contribution.

Composers have shown themselves aware of the problem–too strict an adherence to notation can stifle the spontaneity of the player. Jazz composers such as Duke Ellington wrote music which includes both ensemble playing from the score and sections of improvisation for soloists.

Other composers have been insistent on the details of the printed page, preferring the performer to undertake the role of a go-between communicating essential messages from the composer to the audience. But the world of music is very wide and every taste is catered for within it, whether composer, player or listener.

12. Reading Musical Notation

A further point about notation is necessary. What about the people who like listening to music but who cannot read notation at all? To such a person the complex score of a symphony or opera is nothing more than a mass of squiggles on the page. Does this matter?

Fortunately not! Many music lovers, of all types of music, would be quite lost if confronted by notation. But just as the tourists on an ocean liner need know nothing about navigation, tides, stars, or compasses to enjoy the voyage, so the enjoyment of music need not depend on the ability to read the score. The art of notation is primarily the responsibility of composers, conductors and players.

Admittedly any knowledge of music may help the listener to appreciate more fully performances of any kind, whether live or recorded. But music remains a pure art, filling our ears with sounds that do not necessarily have to be understood in any written form for an audience's ultimate enjoyment.

PART III
MUSICAL FORM

13. Musical Form

So far we have dealt with the background to a composition–its composer, tonality, texture, instrumentation and notation. These elements are fundamental and knowledge of them prepares us for listening to music. But as well as being aware of such things the person who likes music ought to know as much as possible about the subject of **form**.

Expectation of coming events plays an important part in human life. We look forward to holidays, parties, Christmas, weddings, outings, travels, etc. When these things happen we hope they measure up to our expectations which are based on previous enjoyable occasions or on what others may have told us. We know how long each activity will take (with a little allowance either way), what should happen, what could happen and what probably ought to happen and will happen.

At a sporting event the same thing applies. If we go to a professional baseball game we expect to see it played according to the usual rules, with the correct number of players, on the appropriate size of field. The baseball fan knows the rules and enjoys the match in the expectation that this is a properly constituted game. The game will cover the required territorial limits of the pitch and will last the specified length of time. If the players fight among themselves, this will spoil the form and structure of the game and it will turn from one kind of entertainment into something else. All sport, from golf to basketball, from boxing to pole vaulting, operates on these principles–allowing for freedom and variety but within the rules of the game.

Musical form is based similarly on expectations. *The Oxford Dictionary* defines 'form' as 'shape, arrangement of parts...arrangement and style in literary or musical composition'. The composer, by writing in a particular musical form, builds up a sense of rules and guidelines. These may not be as strict as the rules of baseball or football, but the composer still works within certain limits, and it helps the cause if the audience is in on the game.

The composer is a person speaking through music to people. The language which is spoken, like any language, has its rules of syntax, grammar, style and usage, as well as its framework of reference within which speaker and listener can be united. Form establishes the means of communication between composer and listener.

From particular musical forms the listener expects certain things and waits to see if the composer will achieve them. If the listener does not know what to expect something may still be gathered from a composition whatever the form, but less will be received than if the listener understands the language the composer is speaking.

Take, for example, a European listener who hears Indian music for the first time. We will assume that our listener knows nothing about ragas, sitars, sarods, etc. The listener present at a performance may be excited by the color and energy of the scene, the movements of the musicians and the unusual sounds coming from the instruments.

But such a listener will not be able to assess with any confidence the quality of the performance. Many things have been taken in and the music may have been enjoyed, but the music of India is not random or casual–it follows strict forms - and without some knowledge of these rules the essential meaning of the music will be lost.

On the other hand, the listener with a little knowledge of Indian music will be aware of the following finer points of the performance:

1) how each **raga** has its own character (and is often associated with a certain time of day)

2) the nature of the **tal** or rhythmic pulse

3) the significance of the **alap** or prelude

4) the **jor** (an improvisation introducing rhythm)

5) the **jhala** (the exciting climax of the piece)

The music of southern Spain, like Indian music, is a complex art in which many rhythms and structures distinguish one form from another. Each flamenco piece, such as *soleares, alegrías, malagueñas, fandango,* etc., is governed by a separate identity, and woe betide the guitarist, dancer, or singer who mixes one with another.

The Spanish word 'aficionado' (also applied to those who are knowledgable about the bullfight) is bestowed on the individual who cares about, studies and becomes involved in flamenco music; it means an 'informed enthusiast'. The casual listener to flamenco may believe that the music palls after a while because it all seems very similar. The *aficionado* knows that music is like people; viewed from a distance and seen in a crowd people all look very similar–but get nearer to each one and, hey presto, they are all individuals. Form, and an awareness of musical form, is thus a process of individualizing the shapes and possibilities of music.

14. Expectations of Musical Form

A knowledge of form, whatever culture or style of music we are dealing with, builds up in the listener, therefore, certain expectations. These include:

1) Expectation of length

An opera, because of its complicated form and dramatic structure, may last up to five hours or more. A symphony may take more than an hour depending on the composer and the historical period. A popular song would not be expected to last for more than a few minutes. Duration in music is a most important aspect of its form.

2) Expectation of style

This covers many qualities including whether the piece is vocal or instrumental, its sound textures (e.g. melodic, contrapuntal, dissonant, etc.), the use of particular instruments according to period and composer, the size of the piece and whether it is written for solo performer, small ensemble or large orchestra.

3) Expectation of difficulty or simplicity

Some musical forms will be more demanding on the listener than others. Certain types of music will require more stamina, perseverance and tolerance. This is not necessarily to do with length. Modern music for example may leave the audience in some confusion because the music by its very novelty is likely to shock or disturb them into new attitudes. A routine rendering of Beethoven's Fifth Symphony, especially to the experienced listener, (though longer than many modern works) may prove a very easy listening experience. To a young child *any* symphony may seem intolerably difficult to absorb.

4) Expectation of repetition

It is a necessary requirement of musical form that each melody or theme should be thoroughly received and assimilated by the audience before new material is brought in. The process of repetition in some types of music (such as the suite, symphony, traditional jazz, folk songs, Scottish reels, etc.) results in a fundamental architecture of sound to which the listener responds. The psychological implications of repetition are very profound. In many cultures the insistent repeating of short melodic or rhythmic phrases to induce a hypnotic effect on listener or performer is an essential part of musical enjoyment.

5) Expectation of development

Music is like a river or conversation, always moving onwards, prolonging itself in new directions. The longer the piece of music, the more we might expect radical and intriguing developments. The development can also be compared to characters in a drama whose destiny is steadily revealed to us. The destiny of melodic ideas is unveiled throughout the duration of a musical form, and the lengthier works must justify themselves by achieving a worthwhile resolution and climax to the ideas that have been put forward.

6) Expectation of an ending

Just as music must have a beginning, it must also have an ending. The form of music is a kind of journey - setting out, travelling, and arriving at the destination. Composers have given particular care to the shaping of the ending. One work, Schubert's 'Unfinished' Symphony, has attracted attention precisely because it is one of the few compositions which has no ending as such, thus bringing in both surprise and poignancy.

These expectations of length, style, degree of difficulty or simplicity, repetition, development and ending can be acquired quite easily. Each hearing of a composition, whatever its duration or complexity or cultural background, adds to our musical experience and can prepare us for further understanding of the significance of shape in music.

15. Binary and Ternary

Sometimes, for no apparent reason, a tune can get inside one's head and, like an unwelcome visitor, will not leave. A tune takes us over. Whistling, humming, and singing are the first signs of possession.

What are the qualities of this kind of tune which, like an irritating sticking plaster, cannot be shaken off? Tunes such as *Streets of Laredo*, *Clementine*, and *When the Saints Go Marching In*, etc. are immediately identifiable and eminently singable. They are all concise, and the sentiments of the words are at one with the mood of the music. All these tunes use the device of repetition to establish firmly the lines of melody.

Such popular tunes usually consist of either two parts or three parts. (These structures are known in musical language as **binary** [two part] and **ternary** [three part] form.) In many popular standards and jazz compositions of the thirties and forties, composers wrote according to a very convenient ternary arrangement. The tune itself was presented in the first eight measures; this was repeated (just in case you did not get it the first time); another eight measures, appropriately called the **middle eight** then followed, presenting a different melody which complemented the main tune; the first eight measures were then played again. The result was a structure of thirty-two measures, eight plus eight, 'middle eight', and eight measures of the main tune again. For many years a lot of popular songs followed this structure.

In the traditional air, *Streets of Laredo,* the opening statement of melody (A, eight measures) is answered by a concluding section of the same length (B, eight measures), which grows out of and complements the original melody:

The clarity and conciseness of this structure make a tune such as *Streets of Laredo* as durable as oak. This straightforward binary shape welds together two matching units as firmly as two halves of a ship.

A melody in ternary form, for example, the nursery song, *Twinkle, Twinkle, Little Star,* repeats the A section, after a contrasting B section:

From these structures emerges just about every practical musical form. Binary is a logical and satisfying structure, but it is less flexible, less expansive, less capable of development than ternary. In the history of music, binary came before ternary. Western music is really about the developments possible for a composer who uses ternary form. But before the 18th and 19th centuries really showed us what could be done in three-part structures, many masterpieces were created in binary form.

The binary and ternary forms which dominate musical thinking between 1600 and the present day, allow sufficient exposure of the melody for the listener to be fully receptive, and bring in that element of continuity and contrast previously mentioned. From the combination of main tune and subsidiary section come fruitful opportunities for development. It becomes possible for a composer to write a piece of music of satisfying substance which holds together as a unified work of art.

PART IV
MUSIC FOR A PURPOSE

16. Sacred Music

The Church of St. Thomas, Leipzig, where J.S. Bach was Cantor

Music and words go naturally together. The central importance of the human voice in music brings meaning and sound together. Words tend to shape and discipline music. In the realm of song (whether secular or religious), notes written by the composer must serve, support and enhance words. The sentiments of the text should be reinforced by music, making the words more immediately alive and vivid for the listener.

Singers must always be aware of the significance of words. This can only be achieved if the composer provides music entirely suitable for the chosen text. Fortunately composers through the ages have enjoyed the challenges posed by the setting of words to music. They have taken the task very seriously and never more so than when the text in question serves a religious purpose.

From the fusion of sacred words (whether Scripture, Missal or hymn) with the composer's art have come some of the great masterpieces of music. In particular the setting of the **Mass** has provided an extremely demanding musical form for composers to tackle. The five essential sections of the Mass commonly set by composers to music are:

(1) *Kyrie eleison* (Lord, have mercy)

(2) *Gloria in excelsis Deo* (Glory be to God on high)

(3) *Credo* (I believe)

(4) *Sanctus* (Holy) with *Benedictus* (Blessing)

(5) *Agnus Dei* (Lamb of God)

Palestrina's *Mass for Pope Marcellus (Missa Papae Marcelli)*, J. S. Bach's *Mass in B minor*, Haydn's *Theresa Mass*, Mozart's *Mass in C minor, K427*, and Beethoven's *Mass in D (Missa Solemnis)* are some of the greatest achievements of European music. Many composers (including Palestrina, Mozart, Berlioz, Verdi, Dvorák and Fauré), have also been inspired to write a Mass for the Dead or Requiem. This is similar to the ordinary Mass but leaves out the rejoicing of the *Gloria* and the *Credo*. It begins with the consoling words: *Requiem aeternam dona eis, Domine (Eternal rest grant unto them, O Lord)*, but includes the terrifying words of the *Dies Irae*: *That day, a day of wrath, of wasting, and of misery, a great day, and exceedingly bitter.*

An **oratorio**, written for performance in church, cathedral or (more recently) concert hall, is a large-scale work of devotion, putting a religious or exalted text to music. Handel's *Messiah,* one of the most popular of these, appears each Christmas as a regular part of the festivities. Haydn's *Creation,* Mendelssohn's *Elijah,* and Elgar's *Dream of Gerontius* (a setting of a religious poem by Cardinal Newman), *The Apostles,* and *The Kingdom,* are frequently performed oratorios.

Elgar depicted in a drawing conducting an oratorio in 1904 (T.H. Stephenson)

The Easter season presents music of the Passion of Christ. A **Passion** is a setting of texts from the relevant passages in the Gospels or contemplative poems telling the story of Easter week. J. S. Bach's *St. Matthew Passion,* written for an unprecedented array which includes soloists, double chorus, double orchestra, and organ, is the most colossal of these. Though first heard in 1729, it disappeared into silence for a century until brought back into performance by Mendelssohn in 1829. Nowadays it is performed all over the world at Easter time.

Such mighty works must be considered as the equivalent of cathedrals in sound. The effect of attending a great performance of a sung Mass or oratorio is overwhelming. The purpose of sacred music, like that of a cathedral, is to express the highest religious aspirations of humanity.

Though it is not always necessary to share a religious faith to be able to appreciate these immense devotional works, the person of religious disposition may feel more at home with sacred music and its purpose. If we are able to admire both the architecture *and* the purpose of a cathedral, the significance of the place becomes two fold. The intention of a religious work is primarily to elevate both a sacred text and a central belief. Yet even without belief, the works mentioned above offer a Niagaran torrent of magnificent sound. The melodious tumult of choir and orchestra in the resonant splendor of a great church is a very powerful experience.

Hymns and carols, the Gospel songs of the deep South of the USA (from which jazz partly originates), the intoning and chanting of prayer, and the communal music of worship, inspire in the listener feelings not evoked by any other kind of music. Religious music, whether it is Gregorian chant sung by a small choir or the mastery of Bach's *St. Matthew Passion,* unleashes for composer and congregation a dimension of life which is still necessary. It is not so much for *listening to* as for *sharing in*. The function of sacred music is to create in us a mood quite different from everyday experience. For this reason it continues to exert considerable power over the imagination of composers. In the 20th century great religious works, such as Stravinsky's *Symphony of Psalms* or Britten's *War Requiem,* continued the tradition of previous ages. No doubt equally magnificent works will be forthcoming in the 21st century.

Recommended Listening - Sacred Music

Palestrina (1525-1594)	*Missa Papae Marcelli*
Monteverdi (1567-1643)	*Vespers of 1610*
J. S.Bach (1685-1750)	*Mass in B minor* (BWV 232)
	St. Matthew Passion (BWV 244)
Handel (1685-1759)	*Messiah*
Haydn (1732-1809)	*The Creation*
Mozart (1756-1791)	*Requiem*, K626
Beethoven (1770-1827)	*Mass in D, Op.123 (Missa Solemnis)*
Berlioz (1803-1869)	*Grande Messe des Morts (Requiem Mass)*
Mendelssohn (1809-1847)	*Elijah*
Verdi (1813-1901)	*Requiem*
Brahms (1833-1897)	*German Requiem*
Fauré (1845-1924)	*Requiem*
Elgar (1857-1934)	*The Dream of Gerontius*
Stravinsky (1882-1971)	*Symphony of Psalms*
Britten (1913-1976)	*War Requiem*
Bernstein (1918-1990)	*Chichester Psalms*

17. Music and Words

Words and the art of telling a story shape and define many forms of music. Folk song, sacred music, opera, blues, musicals, and most kinds of popular entertainment are examples of what happens when words and music combine to engage our interest with themes of love (or unrequited love), betrayal, disappointment, joy, sorrow, aspirations, hope, despair, etc.

One of the most powerfully dramatic forms of combining a strong imaginative tale with music is the art of opera. Over the centuries opera has developed from being merely the staging of a play with appropriate interludes by groups of musicians which help to create a suitable atmosphere to being one of the most complex and sophisticated (as well as the most expensive to put on), of all musical creations.

The opera composer throughout the centuries works from the text of a play or script usually written specially for the occasion. This text is known as the **libretto.** The composer's intention in opera has always been to unite the effect of dramatic verse with the emotional intensity of music. Thus the quality of the libretto, combined with the twists and turns of the dramatic plot, will contribute immensely to the success of the subsequent opera. But in the balance between libretto and music, it is the latter which will achieve the greatest impact on the audience.

When watching a play or drama of any kind, it seems preferable if the audience can understand the words that are being spoken. But as the art form developed first in Italy (and later in German speaking countries), many operas came to be written in Italian or German, while in the 19th century librettos were often in French or Russian. To audiences who do not speak these languages, some barrier or limitation may thus be placed on their enjoyment of the medium in the theater. In contrast, all true fans of opera would argue that non-understanding of every phrase of an operatic performance does not necessarily spoil enjoyment as the music itself is magnificent enough to communicate the emotions of the action. (In some opera houses round the world, a policy is maintained that operas are produced in the language of the people attending the performance.)

A portrait of Claudio Monteverdi

The first great composer of opera was Claudio Monteverdi (1567-1643), who in 1613 became Choirmaster at St Mark's Cathedral, Venice. Monteverdi also wrote a great deal of church music and madrigals (pastoral songs in the mother tongue, in this case Italian, as opposed to Latin). Only three of Monteverdi's complete operas have survived - *Orfeo* (1607), *Il ritorno d'Ulisse in patria* (c. 1640), and *L'incoronazione di Poppea* (1642).

Part of the dramatic style of opera during the 17th century and 18th century was the inclusion of **recitative,** where instead of the entire text being set to music, some lines are half spoken, half sung or intoned using repeated notes or a limited melodic outline over a simple accompaniment. Thus opera as a medium presented itself as a series of arias, choruses, and set pieces linked together by passages of text in recitative.

In the early 18th century George Frideric Handel (1685-1759), now famous above all for his oratorio, *Messiah,* was the most prolific of opera writers, composing over forty such works for the stage. Many of these dealt with classical or heroic themes, the arias being used to express appropriately deep emotions of every kind, with individual character development of the protagonists being far less important than it would be in later operas.

A scene from Handel's opera Flavio (1723)
(Trustees of the British Museum)

18. Music and Movement

Music without words becomes more abstract and sometimes more difficult to understand. It may make us feel happy, sad, joyous, funereal or stimulated. But a musical composition stripped of the spoken word has no necessity to limit itself to a precise statement of meaning. Music takes over where words leave off and can express those profound areas of feeling that are beyond words.

As well as expressing different emotions, music can also make us get up and dance. The graceful movements of the human body, the rhythms of the dancer, and the stylized routines of the ballroom have always been considered a worthy inspiration of music.

The ballet in a 19th century engraving

The power of the dance was enough for Herod to grant Salome whatever she should ask (her wish being the head of John the Baptist). Literature and legend abound in tales of heroines whose seductive dancing ensnares the vulnerable male, ranging from Morgiana in *Ali Baba and the Forty Thieves* to the gypsy girl, Carmen, in Bizet's opera of the same name. When the dancer dances all eyes are riveted, and music becomes secondary to the dazzling display.

Dance music, therefore, must be simpler than purely instrumental music meant only for listening, and should not distract from the spectacle. The rhythmic movements of dancing feet and body impose restraint on the musician's imagination.

16th century dancers

Historically, dance music is often divided between the vigorous energies of the countryside and the more refined temperament of the court. The essence of a country dance could pass quite naturally into the usage of courtly circles. As it did so, it became more formal and polite. The court musicians tended to polish the rough edges of a dance, making crude gusto elegant and transforming one style into another.

Then, following the whirligig of fashion, dances invariably drop out of popularity. At this point a peculiar thing may happen. Instrumental composers (of whom J. S. Bach is the supreme example) delighted in taking over a dance form where the dancers left off. When a dance is no longer as popular as it once was, it can then be exploited with great success as an instrumental form. Dance styles may endure for a short time only in the ballroom but they remain in people's memories long after their steps have been forgotten.

Modes of dress, etiquette, national temperament and prevailing influences are unpredictable weathercocks of contemporary taste. The rich and famous, especially those favored at court, may influence the way the wind of fashion blows next, but they cannot make fashion stand still. It is instrumental music, recreating the spirit of a dance form, which can preserve certain dance qualities for posterity, captured forever like a fly in amber.

PART V
MUSICAL EXPLORATIONS

19. The Suite

Out of the traditions of dance emerged that most useful musical form the **Suite** (sometimes called **Partita**). The suite reached its point of greatest excellence in the works of J. S. Bach, who wrote them for solo instruments–violin, cello, keyboard and lute. (Bach also composed suites for orchestra. These followed patterns and structures somewhat different from the solo instrumental suites.)

An edition of the lute works of J.S. Bach

As far as structure is concerned the suite is extremely uncomplicated. Out of assorted dances, each with a style, rhythm and mood of its own, a larger unity can be achieved. Put a few of these dances one after the other in a sequence, and they hang together like a necklace of precious stones; each item contributes to the overall effect yet each has its individual identity.

Enjoyable listening to the suite depends once again on expectations. Knowledge of each movement improves understanding. Without some idea of what a dance sets out to do, the effect can be blurred and confusing.

The origins of the suite are believed to be in the habit of pairing a slow dance (with four or two beats to the measure) such as the *pavane* (also known as *pavan,* or *pavana),* with a more lively dance (with three beats to the measure) such as a *galliard.*

Throughout the 17th century composers experimented with notions of the suite. The perfection of the form that we associate with J. S. Bach was not reached easily. Like cards in a pack, the available dances were constantly shuffled. The possible permutations of movements within a suite fascinated composers, who took their time to evolve a suitable climactic and expressive sequence.

Johann Jacob Froberger (1616-1667) is often acknowledged as the 'father of the suite'. He wrote several suites consisting of allemande-courante-sarabande, and others that placed a gigue between allemande and courante. J. S. Bach's instrumental suites, though they vary in actual choice of dances, settled basically around this pattern:

allemande - courante - sarabande - minuet - gigue

(slow)   (quick)   (slow)   (quick)   (very quick)

To this can be added *prelude, bourrée, gavotte, passepied, loure, variations* (known as *doubles)*, and other items such as *scherzo, burlesca, caprice, rondeau,* etc. To the uninitiated listener the suite could become a labyrinth of dance types, each as archaic as all the others. But information about the parts of the structure reveals that the suite is actually a miniature drama containing its own logic.

The opening of the suite is always important. Like the beginning of a novel or film the first moments suggest the mood of the entire work. Whether Bach begins with a *prelude* or *allemande*, an *ouverture* or *fantasia*, the effect is to draw the attention of player and listener. The function of the first few bars will be to establish something of the musical atmosphere to be expected and will also establish which key the suite will be in.

These are some of the usual movements, especially of a suite by J. S. Bach:

Prelude:

An introduction to the suite in a free style of writing with no fixed rules. It is in this way unlike most of the movements of the suite which have two distinct sections in true binary shape. The composer's imagination can be let loose in the *prelude*, exploring avenues not possible in the dance forms which follow

Allemande:

A dance of German origin as its name implies, suggests the fluid smoothness of untroubled waters. Its four beats in a measure give it stability and the number of notes indicates ease and fluency. The pace of this dance is quiet and steady, not brilliant. For this reason Bach often starts his suite with an *allemande*. In a suite opening with a prelude, the allemande provides a useful second movement. The initial qualities suggested by the prelude can be extended by the allemande without giving away too much of the drama.

Courante:

This is vigorous and rapid, providing a contrast to the allemande. From the French verb 'to run', the *courante* is a bubbling, effervescent stream, hurtling downhill. It may not always be profound but it is usually brilliant.

Sarabande:

This slow, stately dance, which probably originated in Spain, is the deep lake to which the running courante often leads! It contains enormous depths of stillness, sadness and expressiveness. Its three beats to the measure are unusual since (like the Polish mazurka) the middle beat of the three is often the accented one:

	>				>	
1	2	3	/	1	2	3

The *sarabande* is the centrifugal point of the suite. To this, all dances move, and from this, all subsequent movements retreat.

Minuets, gavottes, bourrées:

These remind us, in their rhythmic simplicity of the true dance. Their life is very physical and springy, quite removed from the soulful anguish of the sarabande. After the beauty of reflection, they bring us back to reality and simple pleasures. They lack the sophistication of allemandes and courantes, and release us from the introspective gravity of the sarabande.

The *minuet* is a graceful movement with three beats to a measure, sometimes followed by a second minuet. (The first minuet is often repeated.)

The *gavotte* is bright in mood and starts halfway through the first measure providing a catchy rhythm and is also sometimes followed by a second gavotte. Occasionally this second gavotte is in the form of a ***musette***, a dance with a drone bass that imitates the sound of the bagpipe, an instrument popular in France and after which the movement is named. (The first gavotte can be played again.) The *bourrée* is another French dance, similar to the gavotte but quicker. It can be followed by a second bourrée and in some instances the first bourrée is then repeated.

Gigue:

This dance has many virtues. It generates excitement, vigor and zest with a foot-tapping rhythm. Yet its textures are often complex, with interwoven voices, making considerable demands on the player's dexterity. This is where the suite comes to a dramatic culmination. The *gigue* is probably descended from the English *jig*, the characteristic rhythm of which still persists.

In J. S. Bach's suites these contrasts of excitement and serenity, joy and sadness, intensity and relaxation are fully exploited. The assured 'architecture' of his suites and the emotional sweep of the overall design have never been equalled. Bach, above all composers, showed us what the suite could achieve.

Recommended Listening - The Baroque Suite

Purcell (1659-1695)	*Suites* for harpsichord
J. S. Bach (1685-1750)	*Sonatas and Partitas* for solo violin (BWV 1001-1006)
	6 Suites for solo violoncello (BWV 1007-1012)
	French Suites for keyboard (BWV 812-817)

Footnote: Each composition by J. S. Bach has been catalogued by the German scholar, Wolfgang Schmieder and given a BWV number for rapid identification. (BWV = Bach Werke Verzeichnis, Bach Works Index). Other composers with special numbering systems to identify each composition include Vivaldi (Ryom or RV), Domenico Scarlatti (Kirkpatrick or K), Haydn (Hoboken or H), Mozart (Köchel or K), Schubert (Deutsch or D, after Otto Erich Deutsch).

Handel (1685-1759)	*Suites* for keyboard

20. Rondeau, Rondo

One of the earliest dance forms which demonstrates the metamorphosis of musical shape and function is the group round dance. For men and women to join hands and dance in a closed circle is an ancient form of dance. (The accompaniment was provided by the voice singing a chorus or refrain which returned after each verse.)

A round dance in northern Spain, early 20th century

This round dance became a popular medieval form, the **rondeau**, beloved by troubadours, jongleurs and minstrels. Instruments were added to fill out the vocal line and the rondeau ultimately passed from the lips of poets and singers to the fingers of instrumentalists. It became an invaluable musical structure for later composers, infusing the qualities of repetition with new contrasting material.

By the time of Haydn, Mozart and Beethoven, **rondo** (now called by its Italian name) was both a solo instrumental form and had also developed into a useful movement of the sonata. The latter is often described as being in **sonata rondo** form. The pattern of rondo thus became either:

A   B   A   C   A

or:

A   B   A   C   A   B   A

Here, A represents the principal melody, B and C represent the intermediate sections often referred to as **episodes**. It will be observed that the second example in particular has a definite ternary shape. This fact was especially attractive to composers of the 18th and 19th centuries.

Thus the history of the rondeau endures from ancient times right up to the present day–contemporary composers still use rondo form. For the most part, rondos retain a mood of vigor which suggests a legacy from the early dance. Even though the rondo has become primarily an instrumental work, the dance itself survives, often with sung chorus and verses, in children's games, folk gatherings and party activities such as the boisterous 'hokey-cokey'. The magic circle of joined hands continues to fascinate.

Recommended Listening - Rondo

J. S. Bach (1685-1750)	*Gavotte en Rondeau (Violin Partita,* BWV 1006a)
Mozart (1756-1791)	*Rondo Alla Turca (Piano Sonata in A,* K331)
Beethoven (1770-1827)	*Rondo a Capriccio, Op. 129 (Rage over a Lost Penny)* *Sonata in C, Op. 53 (Waldstein),* last movement

21. Theme and Variations

Words and dance, as we have seen, impart to music their own structure. They support patterns of music like pillars in a temple, making the form logical, coherent and strong. But what happens when music relies neither on text nor dance rhythms but goes instead towards the realm of musical sound for its own sake?

One of the composer's solutions to the difficulties of shaping music in the abstract, or **absolute music** as it is called (i.e. consisting only of music with no reference to words or dance movements outside itself), is to write **variations on a theme.** The idea is simplicity itself. To carry out the intention is not so straightforward.

For a start, a composer intending to write variations on a theme should be passionately fond of the melody, whether original or borrowed, and be committed to the theme with a firm belief in its musical possibilities. In the 16th and 17th centuries it was usual to select a stock theme from the popular melodies of the day. In more recent times composers have often created their own basis for variations by writing a really inspired, memorable and catchy opening.

The melody selected should be concise and immediately attractive. If the listener has not grasped the theme by the time it has been played, the variations that follow will be meaningless. This important principle of all musical shape—that what comes first must be absorbed thoroughly to make sense of what follows—is particularly vital in variation form.

The melody at the heart of a group of variations, though necessarily attractive, is evidently not self-sufficient as it would be in a straightforward song, but rather, the starting point of a longer work. The mood is set by it, and this gives rise to a sequence of other moods. Yet, at every moment during the subsequent variations, the listener, consciously (or subconsciously), possesses in imagination the substance of the original tune. A framework for 'free' variations (where no constraints are imposed on the composer's imagination) could be built up in many ways. But in typical variations a musical form is usually along these lines:

1) Following the statement of the theme, the first variation, though harking back to the tune, brings us in direct contact with the composer's inventive ability. Therefore it is frequently assertive and striking. The composer does not need to get too near the theme as we have only just heard it played.

2) What comes afterwards must ring the changes. Variations can come faster or slower, softer or louder, more dissonant or more consonant, near or far from the melody, in major or minor keys. Faster variations may well be placed strategically next to slower ones (as we have already seen with the suite). But each moment takes us further from the original melody in time and distance, and deeper into an experience the composer has created. The theme gives the initial impetus—the variations provide depth and intensity.

3) Within the theme and variations must be a definite sense of progress. The last variation is usually an impressive finale. On occasion it could even be a repeat of the tune itself, the journey then being a round trip, from the home ground and back again via fascinating scenery. But whatever happens we pass through a series of musical events, ranging from the first simple statement of the theme to a deeper process of exploration.

So far the musical form of theme and variations has been considered as it mainly appeared later on in history—as a free structure giving a composer ample scope to exercise full choice in the matter. Composers have certainly taken advantage of the indulgence afforded by the variation form.

For example, Sir Edward Elgar (1857-1934), the great English composer, in his *Enigma Variations*, after a superb and original opening melody, presents characteristic moods and sketches in music of fourteen people (including a self-portrait in the Finale), some romantic and delicate, others lively, witty, grumpy, vigorous, and deeply emotional.

In contrast, Benjamin Britten's *Nocturnal*, written in 1964 for solo guitar, surprises us by leaving the actual theme, *Come Heavy Sleep* by John Dowland, to the end of the composition. The many moods of sleep are evoked throughout the variations, indicated by the composer's instructions to the player—*musingly, agitated, restless, uneasy,* and *dreaming.*

22. Earlier Forms of Variations

In earlier sets of variations composers inflicted a severe discipline on themselves, amounting almost to a musical straitjacket. Freedom of the kind espoused by later musicians was less in favor. The pattern was established in such works by a scrupulous observation, not of the tune, but of its harmonies, and in particular the bottom line of the harmony.

Taking the bass, or **ground**, of a tune, the composer constructed on the actual foundations of the piece a new superstructure. The ground was repeated time after time, and against this unwavering repetition, the composer was invited to pit his wits. The results were often amazingly refreshing and inventive. From the variations on a ground, spring those remarkable species of musical shape, the **passacaglia** and the **chaconne**. (J. S. Bach's *Chaconne in D minor* for solo violin remains the zenith of this form. A splendid example of the *Passacaglia* is the last movement of Brahms's *Fourth Symphony* where he weaves thirty different variations on a theme taken from a Bach cantata.)

The fascination of these more rigid variation forms lies in watching the composer evade the obvious limitations. In using this particular structure, the composer becomes an artistic Houdini, constantly escaping from the tediousness which threatens a musician who dares to repeat himself too often.

Jazz, both traditional and bebop, with its improvised choruses over an established sequence of chords (musicians improvising on the harmonies, not the tune), contains many of the elements of the *chaconne* and *passacaglia* idea. Composers and improvisers through the ages have discovered how imagination can flourish when it is applied to a carefully created structure. Musical anarchy is seldom satisfying to performer or listener. For this reason the variation form, whether free or in the passacaglia mould, will continue to challenge composers.

Recommended Listening - Variation Form

J. S. Bach (1685-1750) *Goldberg Variations* for harpsichord (BWV 988)
Chaconne for violin (from BWV 1004)

Handel (1685-1759) *The Harmonious Blacksmith (Air and Variations from Suite No. 5* for harpsichord)

Brahms (1833-1897) *St Anthony Variations, Op. 56a*

Elgar (1857-1934) *Variations on an Original Theme (Enigma), Op. 36*

Rachmaninoff (1873-1943) *Rhapsody on a Theme of Paganini*

Britten (1913-1976) *The Young Person's Guide to the Orchestra, Op. 34*

23. The Art of Fugue

Certain types of structure in music fascinate composers of widely differing historical periods. The opportunity in such instances is taken up again and again by musicians eager to confront the many skills of their art.

Thus the attraction of **fugue** spans several centuries–a medium which never seems to become obsolete. Certainly the glorious years of the polyphonic tradition culminated in J. S. Bach, the Grand Master of all fugue; his organ fugues, the *Forty-eight Preludes and Fugues* for the Well-tempered Clavier (written to demonstrate the effectiveness of a new type of tuning known as equal temperament which has been in use ever since), and the *Art of Fugue* are some of his greatest masterpieces. Yet fortunately Bach's genius in this field did not inhibit other composers from attempting to write fugues.

The fugal choruses in Handel's *Messiah,* Mozart's double fugue in his *Requiem,* Beethoven's *Grosse Fuge Op. 133,* for String Quartet, the fugue at the end of his *Hammerklavier Sonata,* and the double fugue in the *Ninth Symphony* are some of the finest manifestations of the form. Others include Mendelssohn's *Six Preludes and Fugues Op. 35,* Liszt's *Piano Sonata in B minor* (1854) which includes elements of fugue, Brahms's *Variations and Fugue on a Theme by Handel Op. 24* , and César Franck's *Prelude, Choral and Fugue* for piano.

In the 20th century Paul Hindemith's *Ludus Tonalis* (1942) brings to mind Bach's *Forty-eight Preludes and Fugues* in a work consisting of twelve fugues in twelve keys, linked by interludes, plus prelude and postlude; Dmitri Shostakovich's *Twenty-four Preludes and Fugues, Op. #87* for keyboard (finished in 1951), also provide a significant modern contribution to fugal tradition.

24. The Mechanisms of Fugue

To write a successful fugue the composer must become a kind of musical juggler. A number of melodic fragments are flung up in the air and should be kept in harmonious balance simultaneously. If one tune drops limply to the ground whilst others remain aloft, the result is artistic failure.

The composer begins the fugue by throwing one small melody into action. This keeps going whilst another voice joins in. A third part enters the fray as existing parts continue to wing along. The composer can keep on adding ingredients to the mixture, but like the juggler, the more flaming torches that are tossed up, the greater the risk of disaster.

Fugue is quite straightforward when each part is distributed among individual singers or sections of a choir. Trebles, altos, tenors and basses, interweaving lines of melody enable the listener to hear each voice easily. If the fugue is spread between various orchestral instruments the same applies.

But composers were eager to demonstrate fugal skills in other ways. They applied fugue to solo music, writing not only for organ (which was ideal, having more than one keyboard, pedal basses, and an ability to imitate differing instrumental sounds) but also for harpsichord, violin and lute, with magnificent results.

The inherent problems of fugue composition take us into the realm of pure mathematics. Lines of moving melody can easily collide with catastrophic results. The art of fugue is to write music so expertly that not a blemish occurs. Adjacent melodies must cohere and agree like a happy family, and any sudden quarrel should be speedily resolved.

As a genre, the fugue is elusive and independent, but if a hundred fugues by various composers (and especially the *Forty-eight Preludes and Fugues* of Bach) were to be pinned down on a board and dissected, certain principles would emerge. Over the years an extensive vocabulary of terms has been developed to describe and analyze the fugue.

Fugues have recognizable beginnings, middles and endings, which could be set out in this way:

1) **The Opening** (known as **The Exposition**)

(a) The first voice brings in the theme, known as the **Subject**. This is in the tonic or home key.

(b) The second voice answers the Subject, pitched a fifth higher or a fourth lower than the first voice. While the **Answer** is sounding, the first voice sings a **Countersubject**, a melody which blends appropriately with the Answer.

(c) The third voice enters with the Subject in the original key. First and second voices provide suitable Countersubjects.

(d) A fourth voice (if there is one) comes in with the Answer, once more in the dominant. The Countersubjects sing on in the other voices meanwhile.

One by one, voices have joined the game of fugue. Each entry momentarily hogs the limelight and its individual contribution is firmly established. Once each part has been adequately introduced the fugue can move to the next stage of development.

2) **The Middle**

The fugue now leaves the tonic key laid down at the opening, and modulates to new tonalities. Subject and Answer can sing their original parts in a fresh key, or little sections of music, called **Episodes**, can divert momentarily from the repetition of Subject and Answer. Once the delights of novel material and contrasting episodic interludes are exhausted, the composer can turn towards home and a triumphant finale.

3) **The Ending**

When the Middle stops and the Ending begins is shown by certain indications. One sign of an impending climax might be the return of Subject and Answer in the tonic key. In the Exposition, Subject and Answer were separated to allow each part to establish its own presence. The composer now brings Subject and Answer closer together, a device known as **Stretto** (from the Italian - drawing together). At this point the fugal texture may be densely populated. The voices crowd in like an excitable conversation where everyone speaks at the same time without waiting for others to finish what they have to say. A **Coda** or tail is often added after these final statements to round off the fugue with a flourish.

These are the guidelines of fugue, though they cannot encompass the mass of detail which such a composition contains. It has often been acknowledged that fugue is not so much a form as a texture, the intermingling of polyphonic lines of sound.

Yet out of this clever patterning of voice pitted against voice against voice (etc.), truly remarkable fabrics of sound emerge. A fugue compels the listener to concentrate. Real participation is needed as the ear switches its focus from one voice to another. In fugue the composer is not only a brilliant juggler of melodies but becomes a wizard weaving spells, a mathematician solving problems, and a conjuror revealing amazing musical tricks. Few other types of form make such a total demand on the listener's attention.

Recommended Listening - Fugue

J. S. Bach (1685–1750)	*The Well-Tempered Clavier (48 Preludes & Fugues, Books I and II,* BWV 846-893)
Handel (1685–1759)	*Amen Chorus (Messiah)*
Beethoven (1770 – 1827)	*Grosse Fuge, Op. 133*
Hindemith (1895–1963)	*Ludus Tonalis*
Shostakovich (1906–1975)	*24 Preludes & Fugues, Op. 87,* for piano

25. Sonata

The **Sonata** is one of music's most ingenious discoveries. Like the development of the novel or the camera, it opened up new worlds of artistic exploration. Moreover the sonata was uniquely flexible above all other musical forms in the sense that it could include movements such as variations, minuets, fugues and rondos. Sonata became a recognizable structure with a special identity; composers could adapt that structure for their own purposes without destroying its essential spirit.

Originally the word *sonata* meant little more than *sounded* (from the Italian) as opposed to *cantata* (meaning *sung*). From the 16th century, composers applied the term freely to many kinds of music written for instruments. Eventually however, a sonata began to mean a particular species of instrumental work in three or four movements. (This process began to establish itself around 1742 when Carl Philipp Emanuel Bach (1714–1788), the second surviving son of J. S. Bach, published his first book of mainly three-movement sonatas.)

Before C. P. E. Bach the most renowned composer of keyboard sonatas was Domenico Scarlatti (1685–1757).

A biography of Domenico Scarlatti

Domenico Scarlatti wrote over five hundred one-movement sonatas, set out in two balanced halves, similar to the double sections of a dance movement in a suite. This straightforward structure follows a pattern which served Scarlatti very well:

First half   A section
A strong melody in the tonic key advances to the dominant key by the end of the section. This half is then repeated to give the listener a second chance to absorb and enjoy it.
Second half   B section
The music begins in the dominant key, and moves back to the tonic key at the end of the section. This second half is also repeated providing a structure of symmetry, balance and order.

While Scarlatti's sonatas are now more frequently played than ever, the works of C. P. E. Bach have tended to be neglected by the recitalists of today. Yet the concepts of musical structure they reveal became extremely influential. The pattern of C. P. E. Bach's sonatas set a precedent. He employed three movements which followed a routine of contrasting moods and speeds:

First movement:	**Quick**
Second movement:	**Slow or very slow**
Third movement:	**Very quick**

The second movement was usually set in a contrasting key (such as the relative minor) and consisted of just one section, reminiscent of the freedom of the *prelude* in a suite. This slow movement explored a serious and sensitive mood that did not have to follow any preordained rules. (It is similar to the *fantasia,* a free form also much liked by C. P. E. Bach as an expressive style.) This element of freedom in the slow movement became a characteristic aspect of sonatas.

On either side of the slow movement, the quicker movements stood sentinel. They were often in binary form with each half repeated. Here, C. P. E. Bach sometimes introduced not just one theme in the typical Scarlatti or suite convention, but allowed a suggestion of a second theme to enter. This deployment of two melodies was to set the seal on sonata. Between two themes in one movement, a spark could leap, generating energy and development, fusion and diversity.

A portrait of C. P. E. Bach

C. P. E. Bach's sonatas developed throughout his lifetime in length, variety and sensitivity. As well as the form of his works, composers admired his music's emotional content. The sonata became indeed one of the most deeply emotional of all musical forms. It was the structure which shaped string quartets, symphonies, and concertos, as well as pieces written for soloists and for instruments playing in partnership, from the 18th century to the present day. The tributary of C. P. E. Bach's music thus flowed directly towards the great river of compositions by Haydn, Mozart, Beethoven and Schubert.

26. The Classical Era

The 18th century is the great watershed of music. At that time new textures, new forms and new instruments were developed and the world of music was never the same again. After 1750, the year of J. S. Bach's death, the period known to musical history as the Baroque gently gives way to the era which we call 'Classical'.

In 1749, Joseph Haydn (1732-1809) rented a garret and playing on 'an old worm-eaten clavier' studied the six early sonatas of C. P. E. Bach. Continuity in music is thus maintained. Some quality in an older composer's music appeals to a young musician and teaches him lessons which may never be forgotten. Haydn in his turn was to be the highly esteemed older friend of Wolfgang Amadeus Mozart (1756-1791) and even the teacher, for a short time, of Ludwig van Beethoven (1770-1827). These three composers between them transformed the structure and concept of European music.

In 1755 Haydn became music master to the family of Baron Joseph von Fürnberg, and soon after wrote his first attempts at the **string quartet** (which is like a sonata played by four related string instruments - two violins, viola and cello). Haydn composed over eighty string quartets altogether, a musical medium which he initiated, and which Mozart and Beethoven continued. (It was through the string quartet that he developed many of the principles of **sonata form**.)

String quartets are a musical testing-ground where a composer can write intimate music and experiment with lines of sound. Such music can appeal to players even more than to listeners. If we attend a concert by a string quartet we overhear the music, whereas with a symphony the music speaks outwardly and directly to us. Compared with orchestral music, a string quartet is an economical form of composition, and performances can be arranged with little formality.

The texture of a string quartet is that of utmost clarity and unity. It is the closest thing in music to a conversation. The voices of a string quartet are like independent speakers, each contributing to an overall design.

A book about Haydn, first published in 1902

After a certain amount of exploration in his early quartets, Haydn eventually settled on a four movement sequence. This organization became characteristic and convenient for subsequent composers right up to the present day. The sonata (as it had now developed), the string quartet, and the symphony all follow this essential pattern:

First movement (quick):
The most important movement in that it establishes themes, mood and content.

Second movement (slow):
A lyrical movement, usually in a different (related) key from the first movement.

Third movement (fairly quick):
This consists of a relic of the dance suite; two Minuets are played, the second one being entitled the **Trio** (named after the early custom of using three instruments only in this section to obtain greater contrast with the first Minuet.) After the Trio has been played the first Minuet comes again. (The Minuet eventually quickened its speed and turned into a **Scherzo** - the Italian for 'joke', thus indicating its change of character to a lighter mood. Beethoven is considered to be the principal initiator of the Scherzo.)

Fourth movement (quick, or very quick):
This is energetic, exuberant, and full of strong rhythms making an exciting finish.

Every string quartet and every symphony makes up its own rules to some extent. So if the first movement was not very quick or lively, Haydn could put the Minuet and Trio before the slow movement, thus subtly altering the dramatic shape of the piece. The outline is not a prison for the composer's imagination, but a dynamic framework which expands and lives in response to the life breathed into it. Such a structure offers a composer every opportunity to shape a coherent musical pattern within which many moods can be created.

The advantage of the sonata pattern could be summed up as follows:

1) The composer can use contrasts in tonality throughout the four movements. The home key established strongly in the first movement becomes the foil for tonal surprises, novelties and even shocks.

2) The four movements between them give plenty of differentiation in rhythm and pace, as well as in volume and intensity.

3) Each movement can be shaped individually yet the four movements still cohere through the binding force of tonality and the composer's imaginative moulding of melodic and harmonic elements.

4) The ebbing and flowing of the musical tide culminates in the excitement of the finale. The four movements progress dramatically towards a logical climax.

27. Sonata Form

The first movement in our overall sonata pattern has a form of its own known as **sonata form** or **first-movement form**. Here is what happens in the first movement of a sonata, string quartet or symphony:

The first movement divides into three natural and distinct parts - opening, middle, and ending.

Opening or **Exposition**
The composer thinks of a good melody to begin his sonata. The melody is firmly based in the tonic key, and is immediately significant and memorable. This opening theme is called the **First Subject**.

Between the First Subject and what follows is a short linking section called the **Bridge Passage**; this gives us the clue to get ready for new events.

Following the successful statement of the First Subject, the composer thinks of another tune. This is in the dominant (or related) key; the effect of this melody is to give us a change of scenery and lead us a little way from home. The second melody is known as the **Second Subject**.

The whole of the Exposition is then repeated to make sure that the messages conveyed by the First and Second Subjects are fully grasped. Nowadays, when records and cassettes have the power to give us great familiarity with a work, a performer of a keyboard sonata sometimes omits this repeat. However, the architecture of this first movement form really demands the repeat to drive home the essential landmarks. Without these landmarks the sonata will be less meaningful.

Middle section or **Development**

The composer selects various aspects from the Exposition and explores and elaborates their musical possibilities. The Development does not have to be long or complicated, though it could be. The imaginative use of modulation from one key to another is one of a multitude of possibilities.

Ending or **Recapitulation**

To bring us back home the First Subject is played again. We hear it with experienced ears, having passed through the rigors of the Development. Reaching home after an adventurous journey means that we are not the same as when we set out. The tonic key reassures us that the promised land could be near.

Another **Bridge Passage** eases us from the First Subject towards the return of the Second Subject.

The Second Subject returns like an old acquaintance. But now it is more friendly, being in the tonic key and in the company of this welcome guide we arrive at the end of the first movement. To emphasize a sense of homecoming a final Coda is sometimes added.

Recommended Listening - Sonata and Sonata Form

Scarlatti (1685-1757)   *Sonatas* for harpsichord

C. P. E. Bach (1714-1788)   *Sonatas* for keyboard

Haydn (1732-1809)   *Sonatas* for pianoforte
              String Quartets

Mozart (1756-1791)   *Piano Sonata in C, K545*
              Piano Sonata in A minor, K310
              String Quartet No.17 in B flat, K458 (The Hunt)
              String Quartet No.19 in C, K465 (Dissonance)

Beethoven (1770-1827)   *Piano Sonata in F minor, Op.57 (Appassionata)*
              Piano Sonata in C minor, Op.13 (Pathétique)
              Sonata for Violin and Piano in A, Op.47 (Kreutzer)
              Piano Trio in B flat, Op.97 (Archduke)
              String Quartets, Op.59 (Rasumovsky)

Schubert (1797-1828)   *Piano Sonata in B flat (D960)*

28. The Symphony Orchestra in the Concert Hall

A symphony orchestra performs at the Royal Albert Hall, London (Paul Wilson)

Listening to a **symphony** in the concert hall requires a certain amount of stamina and mental energy. Though smaller symphonies, lighter in texture, are available, larger blockbuster symphonies demand great attention from the listener, especially as their performance often takes some forty minutes or more.

But in the concert hall it could be said that the symphony is presented at its most exciting. The presence of the orchestra, the mighty wash of sound, the fascination of the occasion and the silence of the audience, enclose the listener in a cocoon ideal for paying attention to the music.

The sheer volume of a large orchestra, as well as the energy and variation of orchestral colors, has a profound effect on the nervous system. As the music proceeds through the various movements–quick, slow, minuet (or scherzo) and trio, and the finale–the audience is carried along on a vast sea of vibrating sound.

The symphony concert represents a truly dramatic event. The characters in the drama consist of conductor, musicians and audience, all interacting with each other to provide atmosphere and tension. The dress suits of the players, the movements of the conductor, and the disciplined unity of the orchestra give a striking visual dimension which is very important.

A great symphony is meant to stimulate involvement throughout its entire length. It presents many moods, including fantasy, verve, silence, joy, sadness, wildness and sometimes just good solid themes. The moments of intensity come intermittently. At other times a gentle languor can settle for a short while over audience and orchestra alike, the lull before the storm, or the postlude to passion. In the concert hall the music hits the audience in the face. Confronting the source of the sound, unable to move about, the listener takes in the full experience.

29. The Development of the Symphony

How the symphony originally came into being is a topic much discussed by musicologists. G. B. Sammartini (c.1700–1775), C. P. E. Bach (1714–1788), G. C. Wagenseil (1715–1777), Johann Stamitz (1717–1757), F. J. Gossec (1734–1829), J. C. Bach (1735-1782), etc. all took part in the early development of what we might now think of as 'the symphony'. Taking their cue from the form of the Italian overture with three contrasting movements, they began to evolve a quite distinctive and indeed revolutionary type of orchestral work.

Overtures to operas are works which create an appropriate atmosphere for the drama to follow. Yet, overtures are often substantial enough in their own right to merit performances in the concert hall quite removed from the opera they were intended to preface.

Popular overtures of the late 17th century were of two types–French or Italian. Each possessed three movements, the French preferring a slow-quick-slow pattern, whilst the Italian overture with quick-slow-quick was clearly related to sonata structure. It was the latter which attracted the attention of the early symphonists.

Many composers and many shifts of fashion contributed to the gradual development of symphonic sound. The work, for example, of superb violinists such as Lully (1632-1687) and Corelli (1653-1713) completed the process of displacing the viol as the favorite bowed instrument. Viols, bowed instruments with frets, used in small chamber groups, had been popular for centuries.

Woman playing a viol (Tobias Stimmer, c. 1570)

The steadily increasing predominance of the violin family ensured not only the ultimate departure of the viols but established up to the present day the primary textures of orchestral sound. For the characteristic sound of symphony is essentially the sound of violins and their relatives, the viola, cello and double bass. These dominate the structure of the orchestra, and without their rise to this central position the symphony might never have existed.

Symphony developed as a sonata in orchestral clothing. The typical symphony follows the patterns of sonata outlined earlier. But as well as its musical form, we must always think of its characteristic sound, a quality which pervades symphonies from the early 18th century to the modern age.

Musical structure in terms of movement and theme is at one here with the composer's delight in mixing the tone colors of various families of instruments against the relatively constant flow of bowed sound. In their symphonies composers were able to pursue endlessly the complexities of musical chemistry–the combining of bowed string elements with woodwind, brass and percussion. This process eventually involved a steady expansion of the size, range and capabilities of the orchestra.

30. The Symphonies of Haydn

The first great composer to write powerfully in symphonic form was Joseph Haydn, often called the 'father of the symphony'. His creative support for the newly fledged symphony helped the form find its musical feet. He wrote no less than 104 symphonies, thereby setting an influential precedent for other composers.

These symphonies established for all time the basic ground rules for the structure. Haydn's symphonic masterpieces are four movement works of great variety and vivacity. Apart from an occasional slow introduction which precedes the quick first movement, a device intended to capture the audience's attention, Haydn's symphonies follow the patterns of the sonata and string quartet. His symphonies have often been given picturesque titles as these examples show:

Symphony No. 45 in F sharp minor (The Farewell): in the last movement of this work each musician in turn stops playing and may even leave the platform.

Symphony No. 94 in G (The Surprise): a sudden very loud chord surprises the gentle flow of the opening of the slow movement.

Symphony No. 100 in G (The Military): this is one of the so-called Salomon symphonies and the work includes a military sounding trumpet, bass drum, etc. (Salomon was a concert promoter who lived in London and organized Haydn's visits to England. The twelve symphonies Haydn wrote for these occasions are known as the Salomon symphonies.)

Symphony No. 101 in D (The Clock): the ticking of a clock is suggested in the slow movement.

Symphony No. 103 in E flat (The Drum-Roll): this symphony opens with a roll on the kettledrum.

Haydn's symphonies are energetic and witty, as well as beautiful and serene. They are more compact and succinct than some of the longer symphonies of later composers and as superbly enjoyable music they will hold their esteemed place among works frequently performed and recorded as long as symphony orchestras continue to exist.

31. The Symphonies of Mozart and Beethoven

The symphonies of Wolfgang Amadeus Mozart (over forty in number) create a somewhat different frame of mind from those of Haydn. The profound expressiveness of the symphony is fully exploited by Mozart with more disturbing undercurrents than we normally associate with Haydn. On the surface Mozart's music may seem as smooth and perfect as a sparkling sea but beneath that elegant exterior there is an underlying seriousness and sometimes a sense of tragedy.

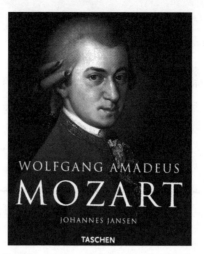

A portrait of Mozart on one of the many books about his life

Haydn blueprinted and established the great musical machine known as 'symphony', but Mozart fine-tuned it and made it capable of a greater emotional charge. Mozart poured light and shade, tension and vigor, anguish and brilliance, into the symphonic mould. His symphonies opened up new dimensions and expanded musical horizons.

For the public at large, Ludwig van Beethoven (1770–1827) remains the supreme symphonist. His symphonies are bigger, louder and longer than those of either Haydn or Mozart, and also fewer in number, being restricted to the magical figure of nine.

Following the success of his first two symphonies, *Symphony No. 1 in C major* (1800), and *Symphony No. 2 in D major* (1802), Beethoven's *Symphony No. 3 in E flat* (known as the *Eroica),* is on a truly heroic scale. It contains a somber Funeral March, and an impulsive Scherzo, while the Finale combines variation and fugue forms. Meanwhile, *Symphony No. 5 in C minor* remains the most universally popular of all symphonies. The arresting opening four notes constitute probably the most famous of all symphonic phrases.

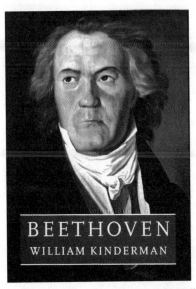

An analytic and interpretative book on Beethoven by William Kinderman

Beethoven's last work in this form, the *Symphony No. 9 in D minor,* as well as being the first symphony to introduce the human voice, is also the most epic. It became known as the *Choral* Symphony as in the last movement Beethoven sets a part of Schiller's *Ode to Joy* for solo singers and chorus. With Beethoven the entire concept of the symphony involves mountainous peaks of human and artistic endeavor. By the time of his last symphony, the orchestra had expanded into a mighty phalanx of sound with a rich array of resources.

Just as J. S. Bach set the highest criterion among composers in his writing of fugue, so Beethoven's symphonies have come to be regarded as the touchstone for all symphonies. Later composers, such as Schubert and Brahms, contemplated Beethoven's achievements with awe and regarded him as the supreme master of symphony.

32. The Continuation of Symphony

Symphony is such a remarkably satisfying musical structure that composers have continued to write in this form. Since Beethoven, the symphonic repertoire has been enriched by many eminent composers, including Schubert, Mendelssohn, Schumann, Bruckner, Brahms, Tchaikovsky, Mahler, Sibelius, Elgar, Rachmaninoff, Shostakovich and others. The great tradition goes on in an expanding universe of form and meaning. The energies unleashed in the symphony resonate still with freshness and revelation.

Recommended Listening - Symphonies

Haydn (1732–1809)	*Symphony No. 94 in G (The Surprise)*
Mozart (1756–1791)	*Symphony No. 40 in G minor, K550* *Symphony No. 41 in C, K551 (Jupiter)*
Beethoven (1770–1827)	*Symphony No. 3 in E flat, Op. 55 (Eroica)* *Symphony No. 5 in C minor, Op. 67* *Symphony No. 6 in F, Op. 68 (Pastoral)* *Symphony No. 7 in A, Op. 92* *Symphony No. 9 in D minor, Op. 125 (Choral)*
Schubert (1797 1828)	*Symphony No. 8 in B minor (Unfinished)*
Mendelssohn (1809–1846)	*Symphony No. 4 in A, Op. 90 (Italian)*
Brahms (1833–1897)	*Symphony No. 1 in C minor, Op. 68*
Tchaikovsky (1840–1893)	*Symphony No. 6 in B minor, Op. 74 (Pathétique)*
Dvořák (1841–1904)	*Symphony No. 9 in E minor, Op. 95 (New World)*
Mahler (1860–1911)	*Symphony No. 1 in D (Titan)*
Sibelius (1865–1951)	*Symphony No. 2 in D, Op. 43*
Ives (1874–1954)	*Symphony No. 3 (The Camp Meeting)*
Prokofiev (1891–1953)	*Symphony No. 1 in D, Op. 25 (Classical)*
Shostakovich (1906–1975)	*Symphony No. 7, Op. 60 (Leningrad)*
Barber (1910–1981)	*Symphony No. 1 in One Movement, Op. 9* *Symphony No. 2, Op. 19*
Britten (1913–1977)	*Simple Symphony, Op. 4*
Bernstein (1918–1990)	*Symphony No. 1 (Jeremiah)* *Symphony No. 2 (The Age of Anxiety)*
Górecki (b.1933)	*Symphony No. 3, Op. 36 (Symphony of Sorrowful Songs)*

33. Concerto

The meeting of the orchestra's symphonic energies and an outstanding instrumentalist is the essence of **concerto.** The **soloist,** a player of extraordinary ability, blends brilliance and sensitivity with the powers of the orchestra. The results are dazzling displays of musicianship by both parties which have justly made the concerto form exceptionally popular.

Originally the idea of a concerto was less favorable to the soloist. The **concerto grosso** of the late 17th and early 18th centuries remains distinct from the solo concerto (which developed a little later). The concerto grosso employed two groups of instruments. One group, larger than the other, and known as **ripieno** (or full) provided the main statement of the themes, the smooth flow of bowed sound being punctuated by the rhythmic and harmonic driving force of a harpsichord (referred to as the **continuo**). The second group, the **soli** or **concertino** added contrasting color and texture.

Among the most famous works in the style of concerto grosso are the *Brandenburg Concertos* of J. S. Bach, while the concerti grossi of Corelli, Telemann, Handel and Vivaldi are nowadays frequently performed. Vivaldi (c.1678–1741), one of the most prolific composers, was particularly fascinated by the solo concerto. His many compositions of this type for various instruments (such as recorder, flute, oboe, bassoon, trumpet, mandolin, cello, not forgetting the four violin concertos known as *The Four Seasons)* were a potent influence on Bach–though it is to be noted that Bach was the first composer of concertos for keyboard.

The 18th century composers (as we have seen with sonata form) possessed dynamic inventive powers. Their development of form was to dominate European composition for the next two hundred years. From now on the creation of sonatas, string quartets, symphonies and concertos would be mandatory for any self-respecting composer. The vocabulary of music with its types of chords, instrumentation and breadth would continue to develop. Yet the ways in which composers expressed their ideas remained within the basic schemes formulated in the period between 1750 and 1790.

An 18th century orchestra, ideal for performing concertos

The concerto is a supreme example of this debt to the innovative talents of that classical era. From the time of J. S. Bach, Haydn and Mozart onwards, composers of all nations would endeavor to do justice to the concerto idea.

Just as Haydn was the principal initiator of the symphony, so Mozart pioneered the concerto and opened up new possibilities for the composers who followed him. He wrote a great number of works in this form, including not only many keyboard concertos (in which Mozart himself was often the soloist) but also violin concertos (again he could be the soloist), a superb clarinet concerto (a new instrument at the time), four horn concertos, a concerto for flute and harp, and a marvellously inventive **sinfonia concertante** (a concerto with less spectacular display for two or more instruments) for violin and viola.

The Greek pianist, Gina Bachauer, performing a concerto in the Herodes Atticus Theater, Athens. Here, the orchestra surrounds the piano like a protective cocoon.

Composers have often written concertos for themselves to play. Beethoven, Paganini, Chopin, Liszt, Brahms and Rachmaninoff are some of the great composer/performers who premiered many of their own works. In other instances composers have become fascinated by an instrument they did not play themselves or by a soloist to whose virtuosity they have paid the highest form of tribute in the dedication of a concerto.

Sometimes composers on presenting a concerto to a player have been rebuffed. The performer concerned may have found the work so difficult or so startlingly novel in its approach that it had to be rejected. Leopold Auer, one of the greatest violinists of his day, considered certain passages of Tchaikovsky's *Violin Concerto in D* (now accepted as an essential part of the repertoire) to be practically unplayable. (Another violinist, Adolf Brodsky, gave the work its premiere.)

For the composer there are specific problems to be dealt with in the writing of a concerto. Not only is there the question of balance, the need to ensure that the solo instrument is not overwhelmed by the great tidal wave of sound from the orchestra, but also the wider question of interplay between the two contrasting elements must be a major consideration. The orchestra is not just accompanying a soloist, but speaking with a musical voice of its own. What the orchestra has to say must be appropriate to its own medium, and yet totally complementary to the concerto as a whole. The soloist must not steal the center of the stage without some musical counter-statement from his powerful colleagues.

34. The Form of the Concerto

Since the 18th century, composers have confronted the challenge of this form. In the process the concerto acquired some of the aspects of the sonata and symphony shape, but necessarily relinquished others. Concertos, for example, are mostly in three movements, not four.

The *Minuet and Trio* movement was probably discarded in the concerto as this dance form was considered rather inflexible in terms of opportunity for solo display. (An exception to this is Brahms's *Piano Concerto No. 2 in B flat* where the slow movement is delayed by the second movement in the form of a scherzo and trio.)

As with all music it is content and substance which dominate form. No overall master plan can be fitted to existing concertos that would apply in each case. Yet, as with other forms, it is worthwhile establishing some guidelines for the inner workings of a concerto.

The First Movement sets the themes and moods of the work. It introduces the brilliance of the soloist and the textures of the concerto instrument in partnership with the orchestra. This can be done in a number of ways.

The most obvious may be to allow the orchestra to open proceedings with a statement of the principal themes. Sometimes this exposition continues for a long while and suspense is built up as the moment approaches when the soloist enters. Once the soloist enters the outlines of melodies so far played can be repeated or the soloist's own voice can be immediately asserted, embellishing available themes or even, in some concertos, launching off into new territory. A feature of the concerto is that we can often expect far more surprises and upheavals in the structural organization than in the symphony. The inclusion of that unpredictable creature–the individual–allows the unexpected to happen.

In Mozart's time this factor of the unexpected was carried further by the **cadenza**, an improvised passage by the soloist during which the orchestra remains silent. The cadenza provides an impressive show of instrumental mastery. This became such a popular aspect of the concerto that rather than leave it to the improvisatory abilities of the individual performer, composers, including Mozart, began to add written cadenzas as an integral part of the score.

What the listener can justifiably expect in the first movement of a concerto is the basic scheme of exposition - development - recapitulation. The things which cannot be predicted are the treatment of themes, the occasions when the soloist will go off at a tangent, and the appropriate placing of the cadenza. To suit the needs of various instruments, composers have evolved great flexibility in their methods of writing concertos.

In the first movement of the modern work the *Concierto de Aranjuez* for guitar by Joaquín Rodrigo (1901–1999), the soloist enters first, thereby enabling the small sound of the guitar to be heard distinctly on its own terms before an orchestral passage is pitted against it. (The same device of allowing the soloist to have the first word was used by Beethoven in his *Piano Concerto No.4 in G*.)

The Second Movement is usually the slow movement of a concerto and this exploits the innate lyricism of the solo instrument. Here the poetic inspiration of the composer gives the instrument the freedom to make its own way, often reducing the orchestra to a gentle accompanying partner. This combination of soloist and orchestra is frequently marked by a singular beauty.

The Third Movement is generally an energetic spirited finale. After the passionate intensity of the slow movement some release is necessary. The composer may well decide to conclude with a rondo or some other vigorous dance-like form.

The concerto ends with virtuosity, vivacity and strength, allowing the soloist and orchestra to reap the harvest of applause and the satisfaction of a brilliant performance.

Recommended Listening - Concertos

Vivaldi (c.1678–1741)	*Concerti Op. 8 (The Four Seasons)*
J. S. Bach (1685–1750)	*6 Brandenburg Concertos,* BWV 1046-1051 *Concerto for 2 Violins and Strings in D minor,* BWV1043
Handel (1685–1759)	*Concerti Grossi*
Mozart (1756–1791)	*Clarinet Concerto in A,* K622 *Concerto for Horn and Strings No. 4 in E flat,* K495 *Piano Concerto No. 21 in C major,* K467 *('Elvira Madigan')* *Piano Concerto No. 23 in A,* K488
Beethoven (1770–1827)	*Piano Concerto No. 5 in E flat, Op. 73 (Emperor)* *Violin Concerto in D, Op. 61*
Mendelssohn (1809–1847)	*Violin Concerto in E minor, Op. 64*
Brahms (1833–1897)	*Piano Concerto No. 1 in D minor, Op. 15* *Piano Concerto No. 2 in B flat, Op. 83* *Violin Concerto in D, Op. 77*
Bruch (1838–1920)	*Violin Concerto No. 1 in G minor, Op. 26*
Tchaikovsky (1840–1893)	*Piano Concerto No. 1 in B flat minor, Op. 23* *Violin Concerto in D, Op. 35*
Grieg (1843–1907)	*Piano Concerto in A minor, Op. 16*
Elgar (1857–1934)	*Cello Concerto in E minor, Op. 85*
Rachmaninoff(1873–1943)	*Piano Concerto No. 2 in C minor, Op. 18*
Bartók (1881–1945)	*Concerto for Orchestra*
Gershwin (1898–1937)	*Rhapsody in Blue*
Rodrigo (1901–1999)	*Concierto de Aranjuez for Guitar and Orchestra*
Barber (1910–1981)	*Piano Concerto, Op. 38*

35. The Operas of Mozart and Beethoven

In the second half of the 18th century, opera evolved rapidly. Nowadays, the great operas of Wolfgang Amadeus Mozart (1756–1791) are frequently performed in the cultural capitals of the world, and his works during this period represent some of the most remarkable examples of his supremely expressive musical art.

Mozart's greatest operas are *Idomeneo* (first performance, 1781), *Die Entführung aus dem Serail (The Seraglio)* (1782), *Le Nozze di Figaro (The Marriage of Figaro)* (1786), *Don Giovanni (Don Juan)* (1787), *Così fan tutte* (1790), *Die Zauberflöte (The Magic Flute)* (1791), and *La Clemenza di Tito* (1791).

A scene in the harem from The Seraglio by Mozart
(Stadtarchiv Augsburg)

Beethoven wrote only one opera, *Fidelio* (originally entitled *Leonora*). This work (which took several years to complete satisfactorily), was first performed in 1805, followed by the premiere of the final version in 1814 in Vienna.

The theme of the opera, a clarion call for political freedom, concerns the unjust imprisonment of the hero, Florestan, and his rescue by his wife Leonora, disguised as a young man under the name of Fidelio. It remains for all subsequent generations a deeply moving and inspiring work.

PART VI
THE 19TH CENTURY

36. Early 19th Century Romanticism

The 18th century developed the great enduring structures of European music. These forms, such as sonata, symphony and concerto, are still used by contemporary composers. Yet in the 19th century it was inevitable that existing forms should undergo extensive modifications and new musical structures emerge.

The early 19th century witnessed the incoming tide of the great movement known as **Romanticism**. Under this influence, literature, the visual arts and music incorporated new techniques and opened up fresh possibilities, gradually eroding the old values of the classical scheme of things.

Classicism could be defined as that which shows a regard for the order and beauty of the classic or ancient world. People imagined that the civilizations of Greece and Rome, at their best, had been founded on principles of logic, reason and balance. Such virtues were admired by the 18th century, and its arts, whether architecture, literature, music or painting, tried to interpret the dream of classical perfection. The classical outlook stressed restraint, rational conduct, self-discipline and the qualities of decorum.

Romanticism preferred to plumb the depths of the irrational and to explore the dark side of tempestuous feelings. The romantic artist wandered 'lonely as a cloud' among the rugged mountains and deep valleys of the imagination.

This brooding aspect of full-blooded romanticism led to an interest in mythology, legend and the cult of past mysterious ages of adventure and the sinister.

To achieve the greatest emotional effect, the romantic composer frequently took pleasure in linking music with a detailed literary scheme or a picturesque descriptive title. Whereas the 18th century, on the whole, preferred its music to be absolute, romanticism implied the creation of particular moods. Music requiring an accompanying 'program' of informative notes about the composer's scenario became popular. This approach to composition is known as **program music**. The technique of relating music to some external event was not new. 16th century composers such as John Dowland had often written descriptive works with titles like *Orlando Sleepeth* or *My Lord Willoughby's Welcome Home*. Antonio Vivaldi's *Four Seasons* depicts sliding on ice, a drunken stupor, birdsong, storms and many other country sounds. Jean-Philippe Rameau (1683–1764) wrote picturesque harpsichord pieces such as *The Hen, The Sighs*, and *The Whirlwind.*

Beethoven's *Sonata Op. 27, No. 2* was entitled the *Moonlight Sonata* by a publisher, a name which has endeared this piano composition to generations of music lovers. Beethoven himself was not averse to a kind of program music –the movements of his *Symphony No. 6 (Pastoral)* describe particular events including *Awakening of happy feelings on arriving in the country, By the brook, Peasants' Merrymaking, The Storm*, and *Shepherd's Song; Cheerful and Thankful Feelings after the Storm.* True advocates of romanticism went even further, focusing on a title, plot, image or basic mood. This concentration on feelings enabled composers to be freer with the formal structure of their work.

37. Schumann, Chopin and Liszt

The supreme romantic instrument was, of course, the pianoforte. By the time of Robert Schumann (1810–1856), Frédéric Chopin (1810–1849) and Franz Liszt (1811–1886), the piano had attained its full span of seven octaves (compared with five octaves during the late 18th century) and its expressive resources were greater than ever before.

A biography of Robert Schumann

Schumann's descriptive piano works such as *Kinderscenen (Scenes from Childhood), Carnaval, Waldscenen (Forest Scenes),* etc., create many immediate images and portraits.

The intimacy of some of these, such as *Dreaming* in *Scenes from Childhood*, contrasts with the epic ebullience of the *March against the Philistines* in *Carnaval*. The listener could find the music moving and exciting without knowing the titles, but the intention is best understood by being aware of the topics portrayed.

The pianoforte music of Chopin makes use of varied forms such as *nocturnes, scherzos, waltzes, ballades, impromptus, preludes, études* and Polish dances like *mazurkas* and *polonaises*. Chopin, often described as 'the poet of the piano', distrusted the more obvious forms of program music, but his compositions give an immediate sense of mood and emotion.

A portrait of Chopin by Delacroix on a Chopin biography

Chopin's application of **rubato** (robbed time–holding back and hurrying on) and new musical forms were indeed innovatory, and his pursuance of chromatic effects (i.e. using notes not part of the main tonality), had a profound impact on musical history. Chopin's strong sense of patriotism for Poland inspired other nationalist composers to seek out the essence of their own country's music. Nationalism became a powerful ingredient in the romantic movement.

Liszt at the piano, in the home of the Wagner family
(etching by G. M. Kraus, Schlossmuseum, Weimar)

Liszt, overwhelmingly impressed by the greatness of the violinist, Paganini (1782–1840), endeavored to exploit the resources of the piano in the same way as Paganini had developed the violin. Liszt proved technically and imaginatively well equipped to do so. His piano works often build up gigantic pictures resonating from some central theme, as revealed by titles such as *Les Années de pèlerinage (The Years of Pilgrimage), St. François d'Assise prédicant aux oiseaux (St. Francis of Assisi Preaching to the Birds), Etudes d'exécution transcendante (Transcendental Studies)*, etc.

Schumann, Chopin and Liszt wrote sonatas for the piano, but compared with classical sonata form the listener may be in for some surprises. The romantic concept of sonata is more arbitrary than that of the 18th century, though the use and development of themes remains the unifying principle. Such devices as the number of movements or the precise organization of sections veer off, on occasion, from the more predictable classical structures of the sonatas of Haydn, Mozart, Beethoven and Schubert.

Of Chopin's great work for pianoforte, *Sonata Op. 35 in B flat minor,* Schumann wrote, 'The idea of calling it a sonata is a caprice, if not a joke, for he has simply bound together four of his most reckless children.' The four movements of this Sonata are actually *Agitato* (preceded by a slow introduction of four bars), *Scherzo, Marche funèbre,* and *Presto* (an unusual and strange last movement, sometimes described as the wind whistling over the gravestones). The third movement, the *Funeral March,* has become one of the most famous melodies in the world. The romantic sonata had thus provided a slow movement of the greatest expressive power, a monument to the genius of the 19th century imagination.

Liszt's only composition in this form, *Sonata in B minor,* lasts about half an hour and is in one continuous movement which falls naturally into three sections that develop his main themes. It is a mighty work combining the demonic, the romantic, the religious and the heroic aspects of its brilliant composer. This sonata provides a powerful example of how established musical forms can be subjected to great changes in style and content.

38. Hector Berlioz

The impact of romanticism on the use of the orchestra can be seen in Hector Berlioz's *Symphonie fantastique* written three years after Beethoven's death. Program notes to this symphony are positively essential. The story is of a young musician who poisons himself with opium. In various narcotic dreams he imagines he has killed his beloved and is executed for this crime. The finale, *The Witches' Sabbath,* is a grisly nightmare in which the image of the beloved joins the horrible hags who attend the musician's funeral.

As well as the scenario, so vital to an appreciation of the symphony, Berlioz makes use of the **idée fixe**, a structural device later exploited to full effect by Richard Wagner in his operas. A small fragment of a tune, a 'fixed idea' (or **leitmotiv** as Wagner called it), appears in all five movements of the symphony, suggesting the beloved's presence. Thus a new principle of unity was introduced into the symphonic form, in which the repetition of a specific theme is linked with the portrayal of events in the music itself.

Berlioz (1803-1869) steps beyond the framework of the classical symphony by using a wide assortment of instrumental colorings and effects. He not only gives the work a striking title but also adds a subtitle, *Episode de la vie d'un artiste (Episode in an artist's life),* and provides a dramatic script. Berlioz enlarged his symphony to five highly evocative movements covering specific events - *Dreams and Passions, A Ball, In the Fields, March to the Scaffold,* and *The Witches' Sabbath.*

An early lithograph portrait of Hector Berlioz

His delight in literature extended particularly to Shakespeare and Byron. Berlioz wrote a dramatic symphony entitled *Romeo and Juliet*, intending 'to write a masterpiece, a splendid new work, full of passion and imagination.' This third symphony of Berlioz involves not only the orchestra but also solo singers and chorus. There are descriptions of the quarrels between Montagues and Capulets, Romeo's love for Juliet, Queen Mab in her chariot, the tomb scene, and a finale of the crowd at the vault, the conflicting families and the reconciliation.

Also inspired by Shakespeare was Felix Mendelssohn (1809–1847), whose overture to *A Midsummer Night's Dream* was written when he was only seventeen. Later he added other movements including the famous *Wedding March*.

Another much-loved descriptive work of Mendelssohn's is his *Hebrides Overture,* written after a visit to Scotland, conjuring up images of rocks, waves and storm.

A new orchestral form was developed by Liszt, influenced by Berlioz and Mendelssohn. This was the **symphonic poem** or **tone poem**, a single movement structure ideally suited for communicating programmatic images.

These symphonic poems by Liszt include *Mazeppa, Battle of the Huns, Orpheus,* and other colorful stimulants to the imagination. His full-scale symphonies bear the titles *Faust* and *Dante. Faust* celebrates Liszt's response to the great drama by Goethe, presenting three massive portraits in music of the principal characters, Faust, Gretchen and Mephistopheles. The work lasts over an hour and makes use of a male voice choir and tenor soloist in the finale.

39. Opera in the 19th Century

Italian opera of this period is exemplified in the works of Gioachino Rossini (1792–1868). His operas include *La Scala di Seta (The Silken Ladder)* (first performed 1812), *L'Italiana in Algieri (The Italian Girl in Algiers)* (1813), *Il Barbiere di Siviglia (The Barber of Seville)* (1816), *La Cenerentola (Cinderella)* (1817) and *William Tell* (1829).

An early portrait of Rossini

The development of German opera and the widespread use of romantic elements was introduced to the art of opera by Carl Maria von Weber (1786–1826), who in 1817 became music director of the opera house in Dresden. His works, such as *Der Freischütz, Euryanthe* and *Oberon*, rejoiced in mysterious fantastic ingredients with magic bullets, medieval castles and the secret world of legend and folk tale. His skillful orchestration brilliantly evoked the atmosphere of drama and myth.

The culmination of German romanticism was the creativity of Richard Wagner (1813–1883), one of the musical giants of the 19th century. Wagner's massive use of all the resources of instrumentation, vocal power and dramatic effect of language, integrated with his themes of myth and nationalistic ardor, establish his work as one of the great landmarks of European music.

Richard Wagner in characteristic pose

In Richard Wagner's operas all the latent trends of the romantic movement find their fulfillment. Not only did he construct a colossal world of the imagination through his operatic representation of the old myths, but his music carries the implications of chromaticism further along the road which was to lead ultimately to the development of atonal music.

Wagner's use of a recurring theme, the **leitmotiv** (each associated with various characters, feelings or objects, such as magic swords, love, sleep, fire, Valhalla, the ring, etc.), throughout his operas was both a dramatic device increasing tension and a unifying technique.

Wagner's extraordinary output of famous operas includes *Der fliegende Holländer (The Flying Dutchman)* (first performance 1843), *Tannhäuser* (1845), *Lohengrin* (1850), *Der Ring des Nibelungen (The Ring of the Nibelungs)*, a cycle of four operas comprising *Das Rheingold (The Rhine Gold)* (1869), *Die Walküre (The Valkyrie)* (1870), *Siegfried* (1876) and *Götterdämmerung (Twilight of the Gods)* (1876), as well as *Tristan und Isolde* (1865), *Die Meistersinger von Nürnberg (The Mastersingers of Nuremberg)* (1868), and *Parsifal* (1882).

Wagner's great achievements in the movement for German national opera were contemporaneous with the operas of Giuseppe Verdi (1813-1901), born only four and a half months after Wagner.

A satirical caricature of Verdi after the first performance of Otello in 1887

Verdi explored unprecedented new horizons in Italian opera with works such as *Nabucco* (first performance 1842), *Macbeth* (1847), *Rigoletto* (1851), *Il Trovatore* (1853), *La Traviata* (1853), *The Sicilian Vespers* (1855), *Un Ballo in Maschera (A Masked Ball)* (1859), *The Force of Destiny* (1862), *Don Carlos* (1867), *Aida* (1871), *Otello* (1887), and *Falstaff* (1893). Apart from his last work, *Falstaff*, a comedy produced in extreme old age, Verdi composed profoundly tragic dramas, full of poignant arias and powerfully expressed emotions, the very essence of what opera has come to represent for the general public.

These great Italian traditions of opera were continued into the 20th century by Giacomo Puccini (1858–1924). Puccini heard Verdi's *Aida* when he was seventeen years old, and decided he would write operas henceforth. He was influenced also in his later works to some extent by the example of Pietro Mascagni (1863–1945), whose opera, *Cavalleria rusticana* (first performance 1890), brought in realistic aspects of contemporary life, including the sordid and unpleasant, in what is known as *verismo*.

Puccini was not entirely a *verismo* composer. But his best loved works such as *Manon Lescaut* (first performance 1893), *La Bohème* (1896), *Tosca* (1900), *Madame Butterfly* (1904), and *Turandot* (1926) were comprised of elements of realism and full-blooded passion in expressive juxtaposition.

40. Johannes Brahms

Some 19th century composers drew back from the imaginative extravaganza of romanticism, seeking instead to preserve classical symmetry and clarity. Of these Johannes Brahms (1833–1897) is perhaps the foremost. His masters were Bach and Beethoven and his sonatas, symphonies and concertos are far from the concepts of program music.

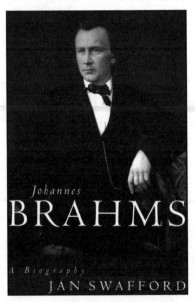

A biography of Brahms

Brahms was particularly fond of the variation form and wrote several sets of these. In *Variations and Fugue on a Theme of Handel, Op. 24* for piano there are twenty-five variations concluding with a titanic fugue.

The *St. Anthony Variations* and the last movement of *Symphony No. 4 in E minor* are fine examples of orchestral writing in this form. Brahms's interest in variation form is an indication of continuity between classicism and the mid-19th century. But in Brahms's piano music we find compositions with romantic titles such as **capriccio, rhapsody** and **intermezzo**. (Liszt wrote over a dozen *Hungarian Rhapsodies.*) These fairly vague musical terms leave the composer enough freedom to invest the form with his own meaning. The *Hungarian Dances* of Brahms, written for piano duet, stimulated other composers such as Dvořák and Grieg to write dances with strong national characteristics.

41. The Music of Nationalism

The influence of nationalism in 19th century music became one of the most potent forces, adding exciting new colors and textures to music.

A recording of Tchaikovsky's symphonies

Nowadays, the popular compositions of Piotr Ilyich Tchaikovsky (1840–1893) represent some of the most vividly nationalistic music of this period. The passionate outpouring of his symphonies, concertos, operas, etc., the intensity of his orchestration, and the brooding introversion of his melodies, are now recognized as the finest product of Russian romanticism. Yet his admiration of classical forms caused him to be regarded by other Russian composers of his time as more 'westernized' than they were. But his music transcends these definitions, and, while being Russian to the core, has proved of appeal to all nations.

Meanwhile the Russian identity of Alexander Borodin (1833–1887), Modest Mussorgsky (1839–1881), Nikolai Rimsky-Korsakov (1844–1908) and Sergei Rachmaninoff (1873–1943), the Czech symphonic poems, *Má Vlast* ('My Fatherland') by Bedrich Smetana (1824–1884), and the Bohemian flavour of much of the music of Antonín Dvorák (1841–1904), the Norwegian voice of Edvard Grieg (1843–1907), the Moravian roots of Leos Janacek (1854–1928), the Spanish evocations of Isaac Albéniz (1860–1909), and the Finnish landscape of Jean Sibelius (1865–1957) are some of the examples of composers who celebrated national identities. They brought together the poetic vision of individual composers with an assertion of the musical traditions of entire nations.

The musical forms through which this sense of national identity revealed itself are many and varied. They range from the operas of Verdi (1813–1901), who was a powerful force in the political unification of Italy, to the *Peer Gynt Suites* by Grieg and the geographical pictorialism of Albéniz's pianoforte music. It was the coming together of so many musical developments throughout the entire 19th century which made such diversity possible.

Recommended Listening - The 19th Century

Rossini (1792–1868)
Overtures: Barber of Seville, Thieving Magpie, & William Tell

Berlioz (1803–1869)
Symphonie fantastique

Mendelssohn (1809–1847)
Overture, The Hebrides (Fingal's Cave)
A Midsummer Night's Dream (Incidental Music)

Chopin (1810–1849)
Nocturne No. 2 in E flat, Op. 9
Sonata No. 2 in B flat minor, Op. 35

Schumann (1810–1856)
Carnaval, Op. 9

Liszt (1811–1886)
Hungarian Rhapsodies
Sonata in B minor

Wagner (1813–1883)
Overture, Tannhäuser
Ride of the Valkyries

Smetana (1824–1884)
Vltava (Symphonic Poems, Má Vlast)

Borodin (1833–1887)
Polovtsian Dances (Prince Igor)

Brahms (1833–1897)
Academic Festival Overture

Saint-Saëns (1835–1921)
Danse macabre, Op. 40

Bizet (1838–1875)
Suites: Carmen, L'Arlésienne

Mussorgsky (1839–1881)
Night on the Bare Mountain
Pictures from an Exhibition

Tchaikovsky (1840–1893)
Ballet Music from Nutcracker, Sleeping Beauty, & Swan Lake
1812 Overture

Grieg (1843–1907)
Peer Gynt Suites

Rimsky-Korsakov (1844–1908)
Symphonic Suite, Scheherazade

Sibelius (1865–1957)
Finlandia, Op. 26

PART VII
THE 20TH CENTURY

42. The Age of Change

The 20th century achieved extraordinary developments in music, art and literature, the extent of which could never have been remotely imagined previously. These artistic and cultural developments were brought about by catastrophic historical events in the shape of massive wars and upheavals, and, in time of peace, by technological innovation at every level.

The impact of history and technological progress on music during the 20th century was crucial. The dislocation and chaos of two world wars, the instability of international peace and the high-speed pace of modern life were inevitably reflected in contemporary art. 20th century music often recreated the hectic rhythms and the sense of disturbance felt by people of many nations.

Never before the 20th century had the experience of listening to music been so easily available. The rapid evolution of recording technology, and the progress of radio and television made music accessible during everyday life in a way that would have amazed previous generations. The age-old dreams of humanity, to fly, to travel quickly and to preserve recordings of living sound, were triumphantly realized.

Music of the 20th century has often been criticized for portraying the harsher realities of modern living. One might as well blame a mirror for reflecting the care-worn lines of a tired face. Though a purpose of music might often be to soothe and distract, composers and artists had to be honest about the world we inhabit. The message from composers was frequently ominous and threatening. But the reality of the 20th century, with its unspeakable horrors of the past and profound uncertainties of the future, was far more menacing than music could ever express.

Certainly in the 20th century much of the popular music disseminated daily through radio and television could be seen as musical tranquilizers meant for mass consumption and intended to lull, bemuse and soothe. The use of multiple violins for background music in airports and supermarkets, the nostalgic melodiousness of daily music of earlier decades–all are bromides designed to induce a feeling of well-being, sophistication and poise. The smooth musical wallpaper of the cocktail pianist, the elegant saxophones of the formal ballroom and the unobtrusive meanderings of a Palm Court orchestra were similar manifestations of a particularly 20th century product.

In the 20th century, for the first time, because of the expense of hiring musicians, the blandness of background music in hotels, bars and restaurants was taken one stage further by infiltrating music on an endlessly revolving tape to provide an inexpensive aural backcloth. In previous centuries music could never have been heard without musicians being present. One phenomenon of the 20th century was to disembody music, giving us background sound but with no necessity to respond to it by way of applause or acknowledgement.

Both jazz and then rock music fought hard against any concept of music as mere ornamental background. Jazz singers traditionally transcended the well-disciplined rhythms of formal dance music while improvisation and spontaneity cut through the subservient role expected of musicians. The style of bebop jazz from the 1940s onwards moved even further, forcing modernistic harmonies and angular cross-rhythms into the language of jazz.

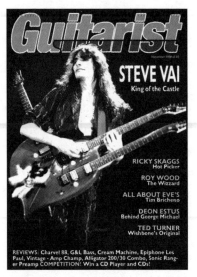

The 20th century image of the rock musician

Rock music from its origins developed in rebellion and dissent against the smooth nothingness of so much popular music of the 1950s. The short-haired, bow-tied, dinner-jacketed image of the dance band musician was replaced by the long-haired, agitated youthfulness of rock musicians dressed either in colorful display clothes or casual denims.

From the late 1950s onwards, rock music evolved its own dynamic vocabulary, communicating with millions of people. Constantly renewing its vitality, the horizons of rock (with its musical structures founded on one or more vocalists, guitar, keyboard, bass guitar and many other instruments, all moulded together by the pounding pulse of the drummer), expanded till the whole world united in listening.

43. Claude Debussy

Throughout the 20th century, composers outside popular music often tended to retreat more and more into their private world. They found it necessary quite early on to make great adjustments to the principles of musical creation which had dominated previous centuries. In particular, composers urgently desired to forge a musical language capable of expressing the new world which thrust itself upon them.

In the visual arts, in literature and drama, intense experimentation also took place. The novels of James Joyce, the poetry of T. S. Eliot and the paintings of Pablo Picasso, are three significant examples of profound upheavals in the textures and structures of European art. Though later these artists were accepted as part of the establishment, their early cataclysmic struggles led to much opposition from the old guard.

The process of radically changing traditional ideas about composition was characterized at the end of the 19th century by the music of Claude Debussy (1862–1918). To many, his work and ideas represent a significant landmark in the progression towards the 20th century musical revolution. Influenced by painters and poets, Debussy brought the movement of Impressionism into music.

In his compositions Debussy sought to give a vivid impression of pictorial images. His titles such as *La Mer (The Sea), Prélude à l'après-midi d'un faune (Prelude to the afternoon of a faun), La fille aux cheveux de lin (The girl with the flaxen hair), La Cathédrale engloutie (The submerged cathedral), Des pas sur la neige (Footsteps in the snow), Clair de lune (Moonlight), Feux d'artifice (Fireworks), Reflets dans l'eau (Reflections in the water),* etc. all indicate the evocative nature of his music.

Claude Debussy

Debussy, by integrating effects such as the use of the old church modes, the whole tone scale (dividing the octave into six steps instead of eight), parallel movement of intervals, the oriental flavor of the pentatonic scale and dissonant chords which did not resolve into the usual cadences coming home to the tonic key, succeeded in refreshing the accepted notions of tonality of his time.

Now acknowledged as a major influence on 20th century composers, his music is much appreciated by the general public. (Debussy's piano solo, *Clair de lune,* has become as much a popular favorite as Beethoven's *Moonlight Sonata.)*

44. Maurice Ravel

Maurice Ravel (1875–1937), a pupil of the great French composer Gabriel Fauré (1845–1924), enriched the artistic palette of musical coloring and imaginative depiction in the early 20th century.

Ravel's piano works lie at the center of his creative output and are not only outstandingly virtuosic in their difficulty but also express vivid images. *Gaspard de la Nuit* (1908), for example, one of the most formidable works for a concert pianist, includes *Le Gibet (The Gibbet),* with its gruesome atmospheric of execution, while the final movement, *Scarbo,* evokes a macabre nocturnal imp. In *Pavane pour une Infante défunte (Pavane for a dead Princess)* (1899), Ravel takes us back to a stately world of dignity and calm, through a blend of a perfect melody and his own characteristic harmonic magic. Equally evocative is the suite, *Ma mère l'oye (Mother Goose)* (1908), originally for piano duet but later orchestrated.

The collected writings of Maurice Ravel

Ravel's most widely known work for the general public is the famous *Bolero* (1928), an orchestral work for ballet. This piece consists of the repetition of a single theme constantly refreshed and made new by the use of ingenious and colorful instrumentation and dynamics.

Ravel's essential contribution to the development of specifically 20th century musical concepts has been aptly summarized by Paul Griffiths:

[Ravel] may represent at its most extreme the tendency in 20th century music for individual ideas to be perfectly self-contained, leaving no room for development. In attaining this ideal he made himself a master of orchestration as well as of his own instrument, the piano, to the extent that many of his works exist in forms for both media, both forms being so well fashioned that they have the status of originals.

(Paul Griffiths, *The Thames and Hudson Dictionary of 20th-Century Music,* London: Thames and Hudson, 1986, p. 147)

45. Erik Satie

The eccentric French composer, Erik Satie (1866–1925) is remembered mainly for his *Sarabandes* (1887), *Gymnopédies* (1888), and *Gnossiennes* (1890), piano miniatures often used nowadays on film tracks for their atmospheric qualities of haunting stillness and reflection. Strongly influenced by painters, such as the Cubists, Satie wished his music to be simple, direct and straightforward rather than romantic in the style of the 19th century or impressionistic like the music of Debussy.

Erik Satie, as portrayed by Picasso, on a recording of his piano music
(EMI/HMV ASD2389)

At the age of forty, Satie studied with Vincent d'Indy (1851–1931), and Albert Roussel (1869–1937), at the Schola Cantorum, Paris. Despite this element of academic training, his radical ideas continued to develop in his own way, sometimes taking the form of giving his works jocular titles (such as *Bureaucratic Sonatina*), and writing music without bar lines.

Satie's deviations from the accepted compositional principles of his day anticipated the work of John Cage and other composers of the later 20th century. Among his modernistic tendencies, Satie experimented (as Cage was to do), with 'space music' – positioning performers in different parts of the hall playing diverse works at varying speeds. He gave instructions in his piano composition *Vexations* that it should be played 840 times in succession. (On 9 September, 1963, five pianists followed these directions and played this piece in relays, achieving a new world record for the duration of a musical work.) In his *5 Nocturnes* (1919), Satie continued writing music made up of the intervals of 2nds, 4ths, 5ths and 7ths, and he also experimented with the concept of *musique d'ameublement* (furniture music), written to be ignored.

46. Serialism

The revolutionaries who created a new musical language were Arnold Schoenberg (1874–1951), and his pupils/disciples, Anton Webern (1883–1945), and Alban Berg (1885–1935). Their efforts were centered on the establishment of the **twelve-note** or **twelve-tone** system. To many people the work of these three is still difficult and even unacceptable, but many creative musicians have discovered guidelines within their compositions of great value in their own stylistic development.

Schoenberg believed the traditional concepts of tonality characteristic of 19th century composers were exhausted and could no longer produce anything except imitations and feeble attempts to recreate past glories. The idea that musical compositions must be firmly in a particular key had been breaking down in one way or another for decades. The freedom of tonality displayed by Chopin and Wagner and the extensive use of chromaticism in the 19th century seemed to demand a new theoretical and practical approach to composition.

Debussy had carefully directed music towards new tonal horizons, but it was Arnold Schoenberg who took the process further. Composers, as has been mentioned, had been edging towards a chromatic freedom which verged on the **atonal** (i.e. music with little or no feeling of a central key). In particular, Wagner's *Tristan und Isolde* (premiered in 1865) represents one of the keenest precedents of atonal elements, while the music of Gustav Mahler (1860–1911), Richard Strauss (1864–1949) and Alexander Scriabin (1872–1915) bears dramatic witness to the loosening of the fabric of tonality.

Thus composers were intent on creating a new musical language – one that could avoid the traditional necessity of writing music in specific keys. But breaking away from tonality completely seemed as difficult as a rocket's attempt to defy the earth's gravitational pull with underpowered engines. It was Schoenberg who finally went into orbit and discovered the secrets of writing atonal music. This was to affect the whole strategy of so much 20th century composition, altering the basis of melody, home keys and the resolution of chords.

The·Master·Musicians
SCHOENBERG
Malcolm MacDonald

Arnold Schoenberg, portrait by Richard Gerstl
(Historisches Museum der Stadt Wien)

Why did Arnold Schoenberg find it necessary to do this? Why was it not possible for composers to go on writing expressively according to the accustomed rules of European tonality? The second question is perhaps easier to answer than the first. Some composers after all did indeed go on writing in traditional styles. But the music of those who preferred conventional tonality is now regarded by music historians and scholars as belonging to the old world and not to the new.

Out of the shadow of 19th century art forms, the 20th century vision was waiting to be born. Composers could cling to the old patterns and techniques or attempt to come to terms with a different world. The new, however, could only emerge through experiment, boldly innovative ideas, struggle and anguish.

Schoenberg's solution to the problems of atonal music was not, of course, the complete answer. But his efforts enabled composers to grasp more clearly the nature of the crisis. Other great creative artists would find alternative ways to tackle the issue. What was clear, however, was that Schoenberg's ideas and innovations could not be ignored. Composers were already fully aware that the old basis of composition was no longer sufficient or satisfactory for their needs. Atonal aspects in music were now so widespread and yet so misunderstood that it became essential for someone to investigate and systemize the new musical vocabulary.

By the time he was ready to jettison the idea of writing music in specific keys, Schoenberg had already traversed other phases of development. These included earlier traditional works as well as experiments in free atonality.

In the 1920s Schoenberg unleashed on the world his new method of using the twelve semitones of the **chromatic scale** as the basic unit of composition. In his method, each of the twelve notes was to be considered as equal to each of its companions; the discipline of the tonic note was now to be challenged. The chromatic scale's twelve notes are as follows:

Twelve Note Chromatic scale, starting here on C as represented on the keyboard:

1:      C (white note) -
2:      C♯/D♭ (black note) -
3:      D (white note) -
4:      D♯/E♭ (black note) -
5:      E (white note) -
6:      F (white note) -
7:      F♯/G♭ (black note)-
8:      G (white note) -
9:      G♯/A♭ (black note) -
10:     A (white note) -
11:     A♯/B♭ (black note) -
12:     B (white note)

Schoenberg's compositional method was first to put these twelve notes in a particular order, chosen by the composer. Of the available permutations for twelve notes (without repetition) there are 479,001,600 possibilities, so a composer has plenty to opt for. When the twelve semitones have been placed in the selected order, the result is the *Tonreihe* or **note row** or **tone row**. The note row is often written out above a composition of this kind.

In Schoenberg's method of twelve-note composition, the notes follow each other throughout the work in the precise order established by the note row. This is known as **serialism**. In works derived from the note row, the individual notes themselves can be of any length, at any octave; the row can be played forwards, backwards, inverted, or transposed. But the order of the sequence is to be kept throughout.

Schoenberg's immediate followers, Berg and Webern, hammered out new shapes and structures within which to deploy this startling development. Webern's music uses the twelve-note system with sparseness and economy. His *Six Bagatelles* (1913) for string quartet, for example, last no longer than three and a half minutes. Webern's entire output is contained within approximately four hours' listening time. Yet he has proved a most influential advocate of the twelve-note method.

Alban Berg found fame with his opera *Wozzeck*, a freely atonal work with occasional tonal elements. The *Violin Concerto*, his last completed work, dedicated 'to the memory of an angel' (the daughter of Gustav Mahler's widow, Alma, and Walter Gropius, a girl who died at a tragically young age of consumption), is a remarkable fusion of a traditional form with the twelve-note system. His other opera *Lulu* has proved in recent years to be a powerful dramatic success.

Most leading composers of the 20th century have needed to confront the problems and possibilities of atonality. This does not mean that they all chose or admired Schoenberg's solution of serialism.

47. Spanish Music

The concepts of Romanticism remained an immediate form of expressiveness to Spanish composers in the 20th century. For both historical and geographical reasons, Spain was a deeply conservative country. Thus the leading Spanish composers, even when they studied in Paris (as so many did), tended to absorb modern influences but without pursuing the avant-garde.

For their primary inspiration the major Spanish musicians of the early 20th century found themselves far more attracted to Debussy and Ravel than to Schoenberg or Webern. While Spanish painters, such as Picasso, Dalí and Miró, were utterly in the vanguard of experimentation, Spain's finest composers remained faithful for decades to traditional tonality and harmonies.

The great Spanish master of this era was Manuel de Falla (1876–1946). His ultimate achievement was to restore the identity of his national music, and to do so he often returned to the roots of Spanish folk song and flamenco.

Manuel de Falla

Falla's magnificent lyric drama, *La vida breve* (1905), pointed the way to an art with characteristically Iberian flavor and was followed by immensely popular stage and concert works such as *El amor brujo* (1914–15), *Fantasía bética* (1919), *El retablo de maese Pedro* (1919–22), and his *Harpsichord Concerto* (1923–26).

Falla's views on Schoenberg's serialism were severe:

Schoenberg's music in particular is atonal, and this extremely grave mistake must account for the dislike many of his works provoke in us.
(Manuel de Falla, *Introduction to the New Music,* 1916, quoted in *Manuel de Falla: On Music and Musicians,* trans. D. Urman, J. M. Thomson, London/Boston: Marion Boyars, 1979, p. 21.)

Spanish composers of the next generation most influenced by Falla, such as Joaquín Turina (1882–1949), Federico Moreno Torroba (1891–1982), and Joaquín Rodrigo (1901–1999) steered clear of atonality, preferring to create a vivid Spanish neo-impressionism of colorful images and picturesque evocations.

Though many such works remained within Iberian borders, Rodrigo's *Concierto de Aranjuez* (1939), became one of the world's best known 20th century concertos, its superb melodic lines and impulsive rhythmic drive ensuring an extraordinary international popularity.

Exceptions to the traditionalism of 20th century Spanish music include the Catalan composer Federico Mompou (1893–1987), who wrote exquisite Satie-like piano miniatures and Roberto Gerhard (1896–1970), also born in Catalonia, who studied with Schoenberg in Vienna and Berlin in the 1920s.

48. Heitor Villa-Lobos

The music of Heitor Villa-Lobos (1887–1959), the Brazilian composer, has a special part in 20th century music. As with Falla, Bartók, Kodály, etc., Villa-Lobos went to the folk songs and indigenous music of his country to discover a distinctive identity for himself and his national culture.

Heitor Villa-Lobos conducting

Villa-Lobos's early approaches were refined by a period of study (1923–26) in Paris, where he absorbed the influences of Debussy, Ravel and Stravinsky. In the 1920s he devised the form of the *chôros,* taken from a Brazilian term for a street ensemble. Villa-Lobos's *14 Chôros* range from a solo guitar piece to huge orchestral items.

Later he wrote his *Bachianas Brasileiras,* an attempt at fusing a homage to Bach with the essential qualities of Brazilian music. (These include the most popular, No. 8, written for soprano and eight cellos.) Villa-Lobos wrote hundreds of pieces and, like Kodály, became a massive presence in the musical education of his country. He will also be especially remembered for his guitar music such as *Twelve Studies* (1929), *Five Preludes* (c. 1940), and a *Guitar Concerto* (1951) as well as a quantity of beautiful piano music.

49. Through Folk Songs to the 20th Century

Béla Bartók (1881–1945) is an example of a 20th century composer who found artistic fulfillment in a very different way from Schoenberg. Bartók developed an original contemporary musical language entirely his own, incorporating exotic scales and vigorous rhythms, after a long study of Hungarian and Romanian folk music. (Throughout his life he collected several thousand songs!)

In his *Autobiography* (1921), Bartók commented:

The study of all this peasant music had the decisive significance for me that it led to the possibility of a complete emancipation from the exclusive rule of the major-minor system. For the overwhelming proportion of the repertory of melodies, and the most valuable of them, adhere to the old church modes or the ancient Greek modes and certain still older modes (especially pentatonic)...Thus it was clear that the old scales, disused in our art-music, had by no means lost their vitality. Returning to their use made possible novel harmonic combinations. This treatment of the diatonic scale led to liberation from the rigid major-minor scale and finally to the completely free availability of every single note of our chromatic twelve-note system.
(Quoted in W. Austin, *Music in the 20th Century,* Dent, 1966, p. 226.)

BARTÓK
his life and times
HAMISH MILNE

A short biography of Béla Bartók

Thus Bartók was seeking a similar freedom from the tyranny of the traditional major-minor scales to that of Schoenberg, but by another route and therefore his compositions sound very different indeed. At the same time as Bartók absorbed and transmuted the rich material of folk cultures, he made use of the classical forms of European music, such as the string quartet and concerto.

Zoltán Kodály (1882–1967), a fellow Hungarian and close friend of Bartók, also assembled a huge collection of folk songs. His energies were similarly mobilized in the cause of musical education, establishing a progressive syllabus of graded teaching throughout the schools of Hungary and inspiring disciples of the method worldwide.

Kodály's best known compositions include *Psalmus Hungaricus* (1923), commemorating the half-century of the union of Buda and Pest, the orchestral suite (originally a ballad opera), *Háry János* (1926), and two further suites of folk dances in modern arrangements, *Dances of Marosszék* (1930) and *Dances of Galánta* (1933). His output of orchestral, chamber music, choral and piano works was truly prolific.

Less experimental than Bartók, Kodály rooted his music in concepts of traditional tonality and rhythmic meter, expressing in his own terms the hopes and aspirations of an entire nation throughout a painful and crucial historical period.

50. The Genius of Stravinsky

Igor Stravinsky (1882–1971) met every aspect of 20th century musical development head on. His output spans the range of stylistic and technical innovations of the changing decades. In this respect Stravinsky's prolific artistry is comparable with Picasso; these two great figures towered over their respective territories and established a unique dominance. The sixty years of Stravinsky's musical creativity include ballets, *The Firebird* (1910), *Petrushka* (1911) and *The Rite of Spring* (1913), operas, *Oedipus Rex* (1927) and *The Rake's Progress* (1951), and many songs, symphonies, concertos and chamber works.

While Schoenberg had developed experiments with pitch and the tone row, Stravinsky was revolutionary in his use of rhythm. His music with its violently colorful rhythmic impulses and spectacular orchestration burst on the public like a hurricane. The premiere of *The Rite of Spring* in 1913 caused an uproar of protest in the theater.

Stravinsky featured in the Master Musicians series

A few years later Stravinsky turned to **neoclassicism**, a movement which sought the inner spirit and meaning of 18th century ideals, particularly in respect of clarity of texture and formal balance. This was a reaction to the lush extravagances of late romanticism. Later in his life Stravinsky fell under the spell of serialism, inspired by the example of Webern. Like Picasso in art, Stravinsky's work covered the whole gamut of 20th century musical techniques in an astonishing panorama of imagination and prolific creativity.

51. Composers and Dictators

Born thirteen years after Stravinsky, Paul Hindemith (1895–1963) was also drawn to the concept of neoclassicism. He wished to lessen the misunderstanding which sometimes separated composer from audience so began to write a wide variety of works designed to be played by amateur musicians. This became known as **Gebrauchsmusik** (music for use). Hindemith was concerned not only with composition but also with teaching and expounding his musical ideas. His book, *The Craft of Musical Composition*, sets out his beliefs and theories on reconciling traditional tonality with contemporary trends.

The banning of Hindemith's compositions in Nazi Germany (along with those of Schoenberg, Berg and Webern), caused him to settle for a while in the United States, returning to Europe after the war.

Totalitarian regimes reacted strongly against experimentation and expressiveness in music, literature and the visual arts. The authorities in countries under communism or fascism usually preferred their art, whether music, literature, painting or sculpture, to be old-fashioned appeals to simple virtues depicting patriotic people happy in their work and content with things as they were. Art and its messages were intended to consolidate the party line, not to challenge or disturb in any way.

Russian artists throughout the communist regime, for example, suffered rampant interference with their creative work, and balanced this against whatever freedom of expression they could get away with. Composers, writers, and painters had to pay considerable attention to the ignorant prejudices of the ruling bureaucrats. To cause offense to the state apparatus could mean either total deprivation of means of income, imprisonment, or (as happened particularly to writers) exile in Siberia.

Great Russian composers such as Sergei Prokofiev (1891–1953) and Dmitri Shostakovich (1906–1975) experienced the heavy pressure of censorship on frequent occasions. Prokofiev, for example, fell afoul of the Communist Party's cultural policy in 1948:

Prokofiev was branded a 'formalist', a term that struck terror into the hearts of all Soviet artists during the last five years of Stalin's reign. Originally, 'formalism' applied to art that was excessively concerned with technique and insufficiently concerned with uplifting ideological content. As time went on, however, 'formalism' came to mean 'anti-Soviet' or unpatriotic. In music, 'formalism' tended to mean simply any hint of atonality or prominent dissonance, or an absence of immediately recognizable melody. (Harlow Robinson, *Sergei Prokofiev: A Biography,* London: Robert Hale, 1987, p. 472.)

Thus in the development of 20th century music in Russia, the inclusion of modernistic elements such as dissonance, atonality, or even a lack of melody, could lead to extraordinary measures of punishment against individual composers.

How such creative artists would have developed if left entirely to their own devices is naturally impossible to estimate. As it happened, to their eternal credit, both Prokofiev and Shostakovich nobly continued the traditions of symphony, ballet and opera, as well as chamber and instrumental works, despite the many difficulties imposed by a totalitarian state.

52. Charles Ives

The United States produced a remarkable compendium of 20th century so-called 'serious' compositions, while the glittering history of blues, jazz, rock and popular entertainment increasingly expressed the aspirations of millions of people, influencing the musical culture of all corners of the globe.

Charles Ives depicted on a recording of his Symphonies Nos 2 & 3
(John Herrick Jackson Music Library, Yale University)

Often acknowledged as the first great American composer and a pioneer of modernism was Charles Ives (1874–1954), born in Danbury, Connecticut. Ives worked for some years in the insurance business, with music as an activity carried on in his spare time. This gave the fiercely individualistic composer total freedom to experiment with a variety of compositional techniques.

Such technical devices included copious quotations from popular melodies, polyrhythms (e.g. two different sections of an orchestra playing in different tempos at the same time), harmony in fourths or whole tones (as opposed to traditional harmony founded in thirds, sixths, etc.), serialism, chord clusters, improvisation, and regrouping instruments in an ensemble in various parts of the auditorium.

Ives's prolific output includes four symphonies, a range of piano works (notably the *Second Piano Sonata [Concord]*, first performed a quarter of a century after its composition), several string quartets and other chamber music, a great number of songs and many orchestral and choral works.

The conductor, Michael Tilson Thomas, sees Charles Ives and his music as essentially romantic:

He was a Romantic composer with an important spiritual statement to make. His polyrhythms, 'dissonance', etc., were only parts of the ever more adventurous techniques he used in getting closer to the specific streams of mind and soul he sought to communicate–the soul of America itself.

(Notes by Michael Tilson Thomas for the recording of Charles Ives - *Symphonies Nos 2 & 3,* Sony SK46440, 1982.)

Other distinguished American composers born during the 19th century include Carl Ruggles (1876–1971), Edgard Varèse (1883–1965, French by birth, US citizenship in 1926), Walter Piston (1894–1976), Roger Sessions (1896–1985), Virgil Thomson (1896–1989), Henry Cowell (1897–1965), George Gershwin (1898–1937), and Roy Harris (1898–1979).

53. Edgard Varèse

Edgard Varèse (1883–1965) was born in France and later settled in New York, apart from a temporary return to Paris (1928–1933). He was a truly revolutionary composer, eager to explore every new sound possibility. His use in the 1920s of unpitched percussion, atonality without serialism, and an avoidance of harmonic and melodic content went further than any of his fellow composers at the time.

Varèse's experiments at first met with abusive opposition from both audiences and critics. At the premiere of *Hyperprism* (1923) for wind instruments and percussion, one critic thought it recalled 'election night, a menagerie or two and a catastrophe in a boiler factory'. *Octandre* (1924) caused W. J.Henderson to comment, 'It was not in any key, not even in no key. It was just a ribald outbreak of noise'.

Another critic considered that *Amériques* (1926) evoked 'the progress of a terrible fire in one of our larger zoos'. In the 1950s Varèse, always interested in the development of new instrumental sonorities, became a passionate advocate of electronic music and the use of tape recorders in composition.

Towards the end of his life Varèse's music received many performances and he was frequently honored by universities and academies for his contribution to 20th century music. However, his fourteen surviving works are generally little known and his significance remains in his potent influence on a later generation of avant-garde composers.

54. George Gershwin

George Gershwin at the keyboard

George Gershwin (1898–1937) has, over the years, reached the widest international public. A brilliant pianist, Gershwin's melodic gifts soon established his fame (at nineteen he wrote *Swanee,* which sold two and a quarter million phonograph recordings!). His music wonderfully creates a fusion of jazz and more traditional elements, of which *Rhapsody in Blue* (premiered in 1924), a piano concerto, is one of the finest examples. In 1934 Gershwin composed variations for piano and orchestra on his celebrated number, *I Got Rhythm,* and the following year his opera, *Porgy and Bess,* was performed in Boston and New York.

Gershwin's early death at the age of thirty-eight was a tragic loss. Yet year by year since that time his reputation as one of the most fascinating and attractive composers of the 20th century has been enhanced by performances and recordings.

His many great songs, including *The Man I Love, Summertime, 'S Wonderful, Somebody Loves Me, Love Walked In,* and *Someone to Watch Over Me,* have been sung by the most eminent popular singers and also absorbed as an integral part of the jazz repertory as a basis for improvisation.

55. Aaron Copland and Samuel Barber

Aaron Copland (1900–1990), born in Brooklyn, the son of Jewish emigrants from Lithuanian Russia, represents for many the central authoritative voice of 20th century American 'classical' music. He studied with Nadia Boulanger in France in the early 1920s, being influenced during this formative period of his life by composers such as Stravinsky, Prokofiev and Milhaud. Copland's early works, including his *Symphony for Organ and Orchestra* (1924), *Music for the Theater* (1925), and *Piano Variations* (1930) were experimental, often showing the influence of blues and jazz as well as European avant-garde concepts.

The second phase of Copland's music involved a change towards a more accessible style of writing to close the gap between the 'music-loving public and the living composer'. This brought into his work folk themes from North and South American music, as well as the previous jazz influence. The music of this period includes *El Salón Mexico* (1933–1936), based on popular Mexican melodies, the ballets, *Billy the Kid* (1938), *Rodeo* (1942), and *Appalachian Spring* (1944) (for which he won a Pulitzer Prize), and *Fanfare for the Common Man* and *Lincoln Portrait* (both pieces composed 1942).

Copland wrote various film scores such as *Of Mice and Men* (1939) and *The Red Pony* (1948). The composer also became an esteemed teacher, conductor, and ambassador worldwide for American music. He was awarded the Congressional Gold Medal in 1986.

A biography of Aaron Copland

In 1938 Samuel Barber (1910–1981) became the first American composer to have his music performed by the NBC Symphony Orchestra conducted by Toscanini. The concert featured Barber's *Essay No. 1 for Orchestra, Op. 12* (1937), and *Adagio for Strings* (1936) (now one of the perennial favorites for audiences), originally from the slow movement of his *String Quartet in B minor.*

Barber's other well known works include *Dover Beach* (1931), for voice and string quartet, *Overture to The School for Scandal, Op. 5* (1932), *Symphony in One Movement, Op. 9,* (written 1935–1936), *Violin Concerto* (1939), *Symphony No. 2, Op. 19 (Symphony Dedicated to the Air Forces)* (1943), *Cello Concerto* (1945), and *Piano Concerto, Op. 38* (1962). He also wrote operas, songs, piano works, and chamber music.

A recording of Samuel Barber's music (EMI CDC 7 49463 2)

Barber's music, predominantly lyrical and traditional in both its harmonic and rhythmic vocabulary, continues to reach an ever larger audience. As one writer commented:

Barber adhered unquestioningly to classical forms and filled them with his personal feelings and thoughts. As Barber himself has stated: 'I just go on doing, as they say, my thing.' (Otto Karolyi, *Modern American Music: From Charles Ives to the Minimalists,* Cygnus Arts/Fairleigh Dickinson University Press, 1996, p. 43.)

56. Developments in Italy

In the homeland of the great Italian opera tradition of Verdi and Puccini, the concepts, dissonance and innovations of 20th century music were not immediately welcome and struggled to make headway. However, a number of composers were soon drawn to experimentation and the new challenging vocabularies of musical expressiveness.

Alfredo Casella (1883–1947), who from the age of twelve studied with Fauré in Paris, returned to Italy in 1915 determined to unite the glorious Italian tradition with the demands of the present. In his subsequent international travels he was distinguished as composer, conductor and pianist, as well as a significant writer on music. He set a strong example to the following generations of Italian composers, encouraging the development of contemporary works by organizing the Venice Festival of Contemporary Music (1930–34).

Casella was influenced within his own work by Fauré, Stravinsky, Bartók and Schoenberg as his development progressed through various stylistic phases throughout his life, including romanticism, neoclassicism, impressionism, polytonality, and (towards the end of his life) experiments with twelve-tone music.

Gian Francesco Malipiero (1882–1973), another supremely influential personality in Italian musical life, was a prolific composer whose output included nearly forty operas, ballet music, symphonies, concertos, as well as chamber and choral works. He also researched and edited the collected works of both Monteverdi and Vivaldi.

Luigi Dallapiccola (1904–1975) is nowadays considered by many to be Italy's most eminent 20th century composer. However, recognition came slowly for him, postponed by the cultural policies of Mussolini's fascist government which, as with communist regimes, strongly disapproved of all aspects of the avant-garde in the arts.

From the 1930s Dallapiccola became the first major Italian composer to fall under the influence of twelve-tone writing, though he made various modifications to strict serialist techniques. He wished to preserve within his work an essential lyricism and endeavored to make a success of writing twelve-tone operas ranging from *Volo di Notte (Night Flight,* 1937–39, following St. Exupéry's novel), *Il prigioniero* (The Prisoner, 1944–48) (both short one-act compositions), and the longer work, *Ulisse* (1960–68). He also wrote the ballet *Marsia* (1942–43) and a quantity of orchestral and choral music as well as solo vocal and instrumental music.

His countryman born in the same year, Goffredo Petrassi (b. 1904-2003), composed first in a neoclassical style influenced by Hindemith and Casella, before adopting twelve-tone methods in the early 1950s.

The Italian born Gian Carlo Menotti (b. 1911), became a close friend of Samuel Barber during his student days in the USA, where he eventually settled. Menotti has become famous for his dramatic operas (about thirty in all) as well as for choral, orchestral and chamber music.

57. Olivier Messiaen

Composers working in the 20th century (as with other creative artists such as novelists, poets, sculptors and painters), could be divided, in a convenient oversimplification, into three distinct divisions.

Firstly, there are the traditionalists – composers who accepted wholeheartedly the basis of the inherited 19th century harmonic and rhythmic concepts of music and developed their art from within those principles. Then come composers who, starting from a foundation of traditional ideas, incorporated within their music various 20th century techniques, extending and perhaps stretching to breaking point earlier notions of tonality and rhythm, yet never entirely rejected the cultural perspectives of the old world.

In distinct contrast, in the third category, are the truly avant-garde experimentalists, composers dissatisfied with the tonalities and methods of previous generations. Foremost in this group were Schoenberg and his followers, whose devotion to serialism and twelve-tone compositional techniques drastically reorientated the sense of continuity between themselves and the past.

One of the greatest personalities of 20th century music was the French composer, organist and teacher, Olivier Messiaen (1908–1992). His music is firstly an expression of his religious faith, but also deals with love and nature:

The first idea I wanted to express, the most important, is the existence of the truths of the Catholic faith...The illumination of the theological truths of the Catholic faith is the first aspect of my work...But I am a human being, and like all others I'm susceptible to human love, which I wished to express in...the greatest myth of human love, that of Tristan and Iseult. Finally, I have a profound love of nature...

(Olivier Messiaen, Music and Color: Conversations with Claude Samuel, trans. E. Thomas Glasow, Amadeus Press, 1994, pp. 20-21.)

Conversations with Olivier Messiaen

Messiaen was deeply influenced by ancient Indian music, while his love of nature drew him to bird song which he often recreated within his compositions. The composer's harmonic and rhythmic developments were complex and profound and included some of these concepts:

1) **Modes of limited transpositions:** Messiaen based many of his harmonies on a system of modes of his own innovation with fixed repeated units of intervals, which have a limited number of possible transpositions. The composer used these as essential colors which, combined with harmonies, imparted powerful moods.

Examples of Messiaen's modes:

i)   2 semitones between each note of the mode:
        C - D - E - F♯ - G♯ - A♯ - C

ii)   2 semitones then 1 semitone:
        C - D - D♯ - E♯ - F♯ - G♯ - A - B- C

iii)   2 semitones then 1 semitone and 1 semitone:
        C - D -D♯ - E - F♯ - G - G♯ - A♯ - B - C

iv)   3 semitones then 1 semitone, 1 semitone and 1 semitone:
        C - D♯ - E - F- F♯ - A - A♯ - B - C

2) **Rhythmic innovation:** Messiaen's use of rhythm, influenced strongly by Stravinsky as well as Indian music, uses individual units of rhythmic notes rather than the traditional sections defined by an underlying meter or pulse. He explained his complex rhythmic ideas:

My rhythmic language is precisely a combination of all these elements: note-values distributed in irregular numbers, the absence of equal times, the love of prime numbers, the presence of nonretrogradable rhythms, and the action of rhythmic characters.
(Olivier Messiaen, Music and Color: Conversations with Claude Samuel, trans. E. Thomas Glasow, Amadeus Press, 1994, p. 79.)
(Footnote: Nonretrogradable rhythms are groups of notes of a symmetrical nature which sound rhythmically the same when played backwards.)

3) **Symmetrical permutations:** Messiaen describes this as 'the unfolding of permutations in a certain reading order, which is always the same' *(op. cit., p. 48)*. This ensures that aspects of compositions can return by the logic of permutations to an original starting point.

Messiaen's most well known works include *La Nativité du Seigneur* (1935), *Quatuor pour la fin du temps (Quartet for the End of Time)* (1941) (written in Stalag VIII - A, a German prisoner of war camp in Poland), *Vingt regards sur l'Enfant-Jésus (Twenty Looks at the Infant Jesus)* (1944), *Turangalîla-Symphonie* (1946-1948), *Oiseaux exotiques (Exotic Birds)* and *Catalogue d'oiseaux (Catalog of Birds)* (1956), *Chronochromie* (1960), *Des canyons aux étoiles (From the Canyons to the Stars)* (1974) and the opera *St. François d'Assise* (1983), etc.

Following *Des canyons aux étoiles (From the Canyons to the Stars)* (1974), written in praise of the natural beauty of Utah, the municipal council of Parowan, Utah, named a local mountain Mt. Messiaen on 5 August, 1978.

58. John Cage

One of the most influential American 20th century experimentalists was John Cage (1912–1992), who studied with Henry Cowell (1897–1965) and with Schoenberg. Cage's utterly revolutionary approach to musical composition proved immensely stimulating to many of his admirers. His complex ideas have been well summarized:

He takes each single sound or noise...as an audible event which is complete in itself, and is therefore incapable of development. So there is, in the traditional sense, no melody and no harmony in his music: and not even rhythm as European composers have conceived it – in relation to melody and harmony. Cage merely places his sound-events one after another, and they are related only because they co-exist in space.

(Wilfrid Mellers, *Music in a New Found Land,* 2nd edition, Faber and Faber, 1987, p. 177.)

After early experiments with serialism, John Cage moved into newer and stranger sonorities, with particular interest in the relationships between silence and music. (In 1952, Cage actually offered a notorious work, for any instruments, entitled 4´ 33´´, which for its 4 minutes and 33 seconds is precisely nothing but silence! It has become his most famous work.)

In the 1940s Cage invented the 'prepared piano', in which the strings are mute and changed in timbre by insertions of screws, bolts, plastic, rubber, or metal to provide percussive effects. (Between 1946 and 1948, Cage wrote *Sonata and Interludes* for prepared piano which lasts over an hour.) Cage also experimented during the 1950s with **indeterminacy, chance operations,** and **aleatoric music,** where (derived from Zen and the I Ching, the Chinese book of changes), choices can be made by tossing three coins or other arbitrary means of selection. Cage's works sometimes involve the use of **graphic notation,** a system of depicting sounds to be played within a diagram kit for the performers, invented (and with instructions how to interpret the graphics) by the composer.

From the late 1930s onwards, Cage wrote many pieces using percussion instruments (later a texture of particular appeal to the Minimalists). From the time of his *Imaginary Landscape No. 1* (1939), Cage was fascinated by the use of electrical sound-producing devices, including oscillators, buzzers and pre-recorded magnetic tape.

After the commercial introduction of tape recorders around 1950, Cage continued to pursue his interest in electronic music, producing what surely seemed at the time extraordinary sounds but which are often nowadays heard as a matter of course in rock groups, film music and advertising.

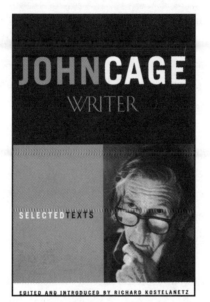

John Cage's writings

59. British Composers

In Britain, significant figures of the 20th century include Edward Elgar (1857–1934), Frederick Delius (1862–1934), Ralph Vaughan Williams (1872–1958), Frank Bridge (1879–1941), John Ireland (1879–1962), Arnold Bax (1883–1953), Arthur Bliss (1891–1975), William Walton (1902–1983), Lennox Berkeley (1903-1989), Michael Tippett (1905–1998), Benjamin Britten (1913–1976), Peter Racine Fricker (1920-1990), Malcolm Arnold (b. 1921), the Master of the Queen's Musick, Malcolm Williamson (b. 1931-2003), Harrison Birtwistle (b. 1934), Peter Maxwell Davies (b. 1934), Richard Rodney Bennett (b. 1936), etc.

Elgar, the epitome of the late Romantic, preferred to shape a characteristically English art from traditional forms and vocabulary. His oratorios, concertos, symphonies and other orchestral works look back nostalgically to the age of a secure tonality. Delius could be called the English Impressionist with his beautiful and poetic evocations of nature in his orchestral and operatic works. Vaughan Williams, like Bartók, became one of the great researchers of folk song, incorporating the energies of its melodies and rhythms into his own musical identity.

Benjamin Britten dominated British music following the Second World War. His many operas and large-scale choral pieces (including *War Requiem* composed in 1961 and first performed in 1962) as well as a wide range of orchestral and solo works achieved international acclaim. Britten's immense love of vocal music makes his output immediately human and approachable. His musical language and diverse achievements have influenced many contemporary composers.

A biographical study of Benjamin Britten

Among younger British composers mention must be made of John Tavener (b. 1944). His compositions include elements of Indian music, the medieval modes, and, above all, the spiritual aura of the Greek Orthodox Church, to which he became a convert.

60. Witold Lutoslawski

One of the greatest representatives of the Eastern European contribution to 20th century music was the Polish composer, Witold Lutoslawski (1913–1994). His music progressed in a markedly individual way, but the early discernible influences on his development included Debussy and Bartók.

A musical study of Witold Lutoslawski

Following military service in the Polish army, Lutoslawski took part in small concerts and played in cafés in Warsaw during the early 1940s to maintain a precarious income for his family. After 1945, with Poland now existing under the stifling political weight of a Russian imposed regime, the composer earned much of his living by writing 'functional' music for educational purposes, films and theater, with strong elements of native folk song and neoclassical musical language.

But he also matured his 'serious' work, completing his *Symphony No. 1* (1941–1947). However, the first Warsaw performance of this piece in 1949 saw him proscribed as a 'formalist' by the Communist authorities and the work was banned in Poland for most of the next decade.

Throughout these treacherous postwar years, Lutoslawski continued to develop his distinctive compositional identity, basing aspects of his creative methods on harmonic concepts which included all twelve notes of the chromatic scale. (*Funeral Music* (1958), written in memory of Bartók, showed the harvest of these twelve-tone harmonic innovations.) Later, influenced by John Cage, Lutoslawski demonstrated his fascination (as in *Venetian Games* of 1961) in the technique of 'controlled aleatoricism', where players are given a reasonable amount of freedom in particular details of performance.

From the 1970s Lutoslawski began cultivating the melodic side of his compositions, enhancing the process by simplifying and clarifying his established approaches to harmony. This served to produce the *Symphony No. 3* (1981–83), a *Piano Concerto* (1988), the song cycle *Chantefleurs et Chantefables* (1990), and *Symphony No. 4* (premiered in Los Angeles, 1993).

Lutoslawski came to symbolize for many the archetypal 20th century artist, struggling to create music against the opposition of terrifying historical and political events and ultimately succeeding in winning an international audience for the profundity and originality of his work. In the later years of his life Lutoslawski travelled widely, both conducting and teaching, acknowledged as one of the foremost composers in the musical history of Poland.

61. Leonard Bernstein

Leonard Bernstein (1918–1990), conductor, composer and pianist, was born in Massachusetts of Russian Jewish emigrants. Influenced by composers as diverse as Stravinsky, Copland and Gershwin, Bernstein's music ranges from Broadway hits including *On the Town* (1944) (which ran for 463 performances) and the perennial *West Side Story* (1957), to symphonies, choral and instrumental works.

A recording of Leonard Bernstein's Chichester Psalms and Symphonies Nos 1 and 2
(on DG 457 757-2)

Bernstein's charisma as a conductor with major orchestras attracted huge audiences to the classical repertory (in 1986, 200,000 attended one of his concerts in New York's Central Park), while television appearances and writings on music enhanced an international popularity. Many aspects of Bernstein, both in his music, his conducting, and his private life, roused controversy. But as one of Bernstein's biographers has commented:

Poet, lyricist, political activist, possessor of wide-ranging interests, Bernstein is to many the Renaissance man his mother claims him to be. And because he understands how to use the media, he has brought music to more people than anyone else.

(Joan Peyser, *Leonard Bernstein,* Bantam Press, 1987, p. 413.)

62. The Fulfillment of the 20th Century

With the considerable crop of gifted composers born between 1920 and 1940 the patterns of 20th century music began to take on a particular complexity. Whereas the developments of the early part of the century are represented by a reasonably small roll call of leading personalities, the period following the Second World War can be viewed with hindsight as a total explosion of diverse creative activities in many countries. The harvest of these postwar years, whether in scores, performances or recordings, is the fulfillment of all the struggle, experimentation and innovation characteristic of the earlier decades from 1900.

The English composer, Reginald Smith Brindle, has diagnosed the dilemma of creative musicians in 1945:

If music has had to 'begin again' at any previous moment in musical history, there could hardly have been such a wealth of alternatives, or so many contrasting and irreconcilable factors, as in the late Forties. Generally speaking, composers were attracted by the works of Bartók, Stravinsky, or Hindemith and imitated one or other of their styles...But with the circulation of Schoenberg's serial music, a seriously disruptive element was injected into the postwar scene and all chance of stylistic and technical stability was lost.

Serialism proposed such radical changes in the traditional concepts of musical structure (and particularly in form, melody, and harmony) that it was completely irreconcilable with the works of Bartók, Hindemith, and then Stravinsky. And so a conflict sprang up between serialism and the rest. (Reginald Smith Brindle, *The New Music: The Avant-garde since 1945*, Oxford University Press, 1975, pp. 3-4.)

Serialism itself was also divided between those who used the techniques of Schoenberg and composers influenced by the somewhat different approach to twelve-tone music by his pupil, Webern.

The bridging of the divide between the varied influences from the early 20th century now had to be sorted out:

In fact, whether they intended it or not, composers of a whole generation dedicated their efforts in one way or another to the exploration of the field between tonality and atonality, and to the integration of serialism into a more accessible musical language. (Ibid. p. 5.)

Boulez expressed the postwar dilemmas in dramatic terms:

In 1945-6 nothing was ready and everything remained to be done: it was our privilege to make the discoveries and also to find ourselves faced with nothing – which may have its difficulties but also has many advantages.
(Pierre Boulez, *Orientations - Collected Writings,* ed. Jean-Jacques Nattiez, trans. Martin Cooper, Faber and Faber, 1986, p. 445.)

Composers from many countries eager to formulate their own characteristic musical language include: Bruno Maderna (1920–73, Italy), Lukas Foss (b. 1922, USA), Iannis Xenakis (1922–2001, Greece/France), György Ligeti (b. 1923, Hungary), Luigi Nono (1924–90, Italy), Luciano Berio (b. 1925, Italy), Pierre Boulez (b. 1925, France), Hans Werner Henze (b. 1926, Germany), Jean Barraqué (1928–73, France), Karlheinz Stockhausen (b. 1928, Germany),

George Crumb (b. 1929, USA), Toru Takemitsu (1930–96, Japan), Alexander Goehr (b.1932, UK), Henryk Górecki (b. 1933, Poland), Krzysztof Penderecki (b. 1933, Poland), Harrison Birtwistle (b. 1934, UK), Peter Maxwell Davies (b. 1934, UK), Richard Rodney Bennett (b. 1936, UK), Cornelius Cardew (1936–81, UK) and Leo Brouwer (b. 1939, Cuba).

As it is impractical for reasons of space to evaluate each of these composers here, we shall look instead at just three of the influential personalities of the postwar period.

63. Pierre Boulez

Pierre Boulez (b. 1925), conductor, teacher and writer about music, studied higher mathematics before becoming a pupil of Messiaen at the Paris Conservatoire (1944–45). His training in scientific subjects influenced his efforts to discover new avenues within the art of composition and he has even been described as the 'musical scientist'. Boulez's avant-garde instincts drew him to the techniques of serialism. In 1951 Boulez wrote *Structures 1a* which approached the concepts of **total serialism**. As one scholar commented:

[Boulez] started out as such a passionate member of the Schoenberg school that he was led to exclaim that 'since the discoveries of the Viennese all composition other than twelve tones is useless'. But Boulez soon became convinced that the same mathematical discipline that governed pitch through the use of the twelve-tone row had to apply to all other areas of musical creation. He consequently developed the serial technique–a *total* serialization of musical means whereby a preconceived mathematical order governed every area of music: note values, volume, density of note sequence as well as pitch, rhythm and color. (David Ewen, ed., *The World of Twentieth Century Music,* 2nd edition, rev. Stephen J. Pettitt, Robert Hale, p. 107)

If this sounds complicated such an assumption would be correct. Behind total serialism is an elaborately complex strategy of musical organization down to the minutest detail. But listeners do not necessarily have to be aware of the theoretical basis behind the creation of such sounds, though it may help them to understand more of what is going on in the music. Audiences (as with any performance) hear a progression of musical ideas producing a pleasing response or not, according to individual expectations and requirements.

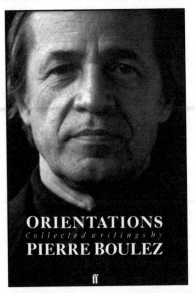

ORIENTATIONS
Collected writings by
PIERRE BOULEZ

The collected writings of Pierre Boulez

In 1955, Boulez wrote what was to become one of his most famous works, for contralto and chamber ensemble, *Le Marteau sans Maître (The Hammer without a Master)* - three songs (on poems by René Char), with six instrumental movements.

Several types of percussion, wind and string instruments (including guitar), provide an amazing variety of impressionistic coloring but the work may present itself to the unaccustomed ear as difficult, discordant and chaotic.

In his *Third Piano Sonata* (1956–57) Boulez composed five movements which can be played in a number of different orders. This led up to the large scale commemoration of the French poet, Stéphane Mallarmé (1842–1898) in *Pli selon pli (Fold upon Fold)* (1957–62), for soprano and orchestra, one of the outstanding monuments of postwar modernism.

Mallarmé's artistic aims of novelty and renewal, quoted here, fascinated Boulez:

...I am inventing a language which must necessarily spring from a highly novel type of poetics which I might define in two words: *Paint, not the thing, but the effect that it produces.*
(Stéphane Mallarmé, quoted in *Mallarmé,* ed. Anthony Hartley, Penguin Books, 1965, p. ix.)

Boulez was equally concerned with discovering a new language:

What I want to do is to change people's attitude. They have inherited their tastes from the past and look only to the past – to museums, as it were – for their music, while all the time there is live, living music in the world around them. My aim is to promote in every field the ideas of today. We cannot spend our whole lives in the shadow of the huge tree of the past...No generation that fails to question the achievements of the past has a hope of achieving its own potential or exploiting its vital energies to the full....The artists I admire – Beethoven, Wagner, Debussy, Berlioz – have not followed tradition but have been able to force tradition to follow them. We need to restore the spirit of irreverence in music.
(Pierre Boulez, *Orientations - Collected Writings,* ed. Jean-Jacques Nattiez, trans. Martin Cooper, Faber and Faber, 1986, pp. 481-482.)

64 . György Ligeti

György Ligeti (b. 1923), a Hungarian composer, studied at the Budapest Conservatory. Living as a young artist under a Communist regime, Ligeti's early development included conventional works acceptable to the authorities and private experiments with the concepts of Schoenberg, Webern and Bartók. After escaping from Budapest during the Hungarian uprising of 1956, Ligeti lived in Germany where, for the first time, he met other avant-garde composers of his generation and attended festivals of new music. He progressed to electronic music and a range of ideas including serialism and chord clusters.

A biography of György Ligeti

In 1965, *Poème symphonique* (1962), written for one hundred metronomes, all set at different speeds and requiring ten operators, was premiered at the Buffalo Festival of the Arts Today. This work (about a widow who lived in a house full of clocks), originated in a story which the composer had read as a young child. The theme of clocks continued in various compositions including *Clocks and Clouds* (1973) for female chorus and orchestra. In 1968, Stanley Kubrick used Ligeti's *Atmosphères* (1961), the *Kyrie* from *Requiem* (1963–65) and *Lux aeterna* (1966), in his film *2001: A Space Odyssey,* thereby ensuring a wide audience for certain aspects of his music. Over the years Ligeti has produced a considerable output for piano, as well as chamber and orchestral works and an opera, in two acts, *Le Grand Macabre* (1974–77).

65. Karlheinz Stockhausen

Stockhausen (b.1928) became a major figure of the avant-garde movement in the 1950s following studies with Messiaen. He strongly expressed his sense of a new era:

I was very much aware in 1951 that I was part of a new epoch; and that an epoch that had started hundreds of years ago, even 2,500 years ago with the way of thinking of the ancient Greeks, had finished with the last war.
(Mya Tannenbaum, *Conversations with Stockhausen,* Oxford University Press, 1987, p. 71.)

His early pieces often used **pointillism** where tones are applied on the score as a painter might add spots of color to a canvas. In Paris, Stockhausen established contact with Peter Schaeffer, the advocate of *musique concrète* (**concrete music** - a collection of musical sounds subject to complex manipulation within tape recorders or electronic devices), and wrote some electronic pieces.

Karlheinz Stockhausen

Throughout the 1950s Stockhausen explored both serialism and electronic music. He also experimented with indeterminacy and wrote *Piano Piece XI* (1956), made up of nineteen different segments to be played in any order.

In *Carré* ('Square') (1959-60), he probed the effects of spatial arrangements with four orchestras and four choirs positioned on four separate stages. *Zyklus* ('Cycle') (1959), for solo performer, involves a variety of percussion instruments grouped in a circle. The player begins anywhere in the score at choice and moves from one instrument to another.

Kontakte ('Contacts') (1960) uses traditional instruments (piano and percussion) in conjunction with electronic sounds. From the late 1960s Stockhausen developed his 'time-space' projects, large-scale stage works involving massive groups of singers/performers, percussion, screen projection, stereophonic electronic equipment, etc.

In Osaka, Japan, in 1970, his musical demonstrations (following the construction of a special circular auditorium), continued for 183 days, with twenty soloists and five lantern projections, each session lasting nearly six hours. (In contrast, Stockhausen's *Helikopter-Streichquartett* ['Helicopter String Quartet'] [1993], requires merely a string quartet, four helicopters, television and audio relay equipment for performance!)

66. Minimalism

One of the last examples of the search by 20th century composers for new ways of expression was **minimalism.** The concept of 'minimalism' was to simplify music by means of repetition of short sections, with 'minimal' slow changes in melody and harmony, both of which tend to remain rooted in tonality.

Minimalism (also known as **repetitive music, acoustical art,** and **meditative music**), was developed mainly by the American composers Terry Riley (b. 1935), La Monte Young (b. 1935), Steve Reich (b. 1936), and Philip Glass (b. 1937), from the 1960s onwards. The influence of their ideas was potent and minimalism became absorbed into the work of various North American and European composers from the 1970s (though it was not always designated by that name). Its devices, to a greater or lesser extent, were also found of value in the creation of rock and film music.

One of the best known and most characteristic minimalist works is Terry Riley's *In C* (1964). This presents fifty-three musical figures of the utmost technical simplicity consisting of perhaps one note, the same note repeated, a six note arpeggio pattern, etc. Each figure may be played as often as desired. Performers are allowed to start at different times. Any instrument (or combination of instruments) can be chosen provided it can sound at the pitch levels on the score. A repeated short note of C gives the rhythmic pulse to the work.

67. The 21st Century

20th century music certainly offers a tangled web of immense complexity. Composers continued to write ambitious music despite the dislocation of war, social upheaval, exile, tyranny and the sense of deep moral insecurity which characterized so many troubled years. The varied movements of grappling with adventurous experiments in sound succeeded in producing many notable works.

Influenced by such a vast range of 20th century precedents, composers of the 21st century will continue to transform our musical landscape according to their own vision of things. Popular music, with rock styles firmly at the heart of stylistic characteristics, will dominate the listening of millions of people for the foreseeable future. But there will also be new symphonies and concertos, new operas, ballets and large-scale sacred works, exciting instrumental pieces and all kinds of chamber music.

In jazz, players will stretch their imaginations and their techniques to the limit. Dazzling musicals for Broadway and the world stage will be written, while film music continues to provide atmosphere and color to the cinema and television screens. Research into the distant past will go on changing our ideas of how music of previous centuries should be performed. New sounds and new instruments, especially in the electronic field, will be developed, adding to the palette of musical possibilities.

But most of all there will be the the the ever-changing revolution of music, compelling us to move into new eras of experience and art. If the history of music teaches anything it is that things never stand still and that innovation and experiment will continue to co-exist alongside consolidation of whatever we already cherish and admire.

Recommended Listening - 20th Century

Elgar (1857–1934)	*Introduction and Allegro for Strings* *Cello Concerto* *Pomp and Circumstance Marches*
Debussy (1862–1918)	*Clair de lune* *La Fille aux cheveux de lin (Prelude No. 8, Book 1)* *La Mer*
Delius (1862–1934)	*On hearing the first cuckoo in spring*
Strauss (1864–1949)	*Also sprach Zarathustra*
Satie (1866–1925)	*Gymnopédies*
Vaughan Williams (1872–1958)	*Fantasia on Greensleeves*
Rachmaninoff (1873–1943)	*Piano Concerto No. 2 in C minor* *Prelude in C sharp minor, Op. 3, No. 2*
Holst (1874–1934)	*The Planets*

Ives (1874–1954)	*Symphony No. 3 (The Camp Meeting)*
Schoenberg (1874–1951)	*Pierrot Lunaire, Op. 21* *Verklärte Nacht (Transfigured Night), Op. 4*
Ravel (1875–1937)	*Bolero* *Ma mère l'oye (Mother Goose Suite)* *Gaspard de la Nuit* *Pavane pour une Infante défunte*
Falla (1876–1946)	*Nights in the Gardens of Spain* *Ritual Fire Dance (El Amor Brujo, 'Love the Magician')* *The Three-Cornered Hat*
Respighi (1879–1936)	*Fountains of Rome*
Bartók (1881–1945)	*Mikrokosmos* *Romanian Folk Dances* *Concerto for Orchestra*
Kodály (1882–1967)	*Dances of Galánta* *Dances of Marosszék* *Suite 'Háry János'*
Stravinsky (1882–1971)	*The Firebird* *Petrushka* *The Rite of Spring* *Symphony of Psalms*
Varèse (1883–1965)	*Arcana* *Amériques*
Webern (1883–1945)	*Passacaglia, Op. 1* *6 Bagatelles for String Quartet, Op. 9* *Symphony, Op. 21*
Berg (1885–1935)	*Lulu* (opera) *Wozzeck* (opera) *Violin Concerto*
Villa-Lobos (1887–1959)	*Five Preludes* (for guitar) *Guitar Concerto* *Bachianas Brasileiras No. 8*

Prokofiev (1891–1953)	*Peter and the Wolf* *Romeo and Juliet* *Piano Concerto No. 3*
Hindemith (1895–1963)	*Ludus Tonalis* *Symphony 'Mathis der Maler'*
Orff (1895–1982)	*Carmina Burana*
Gershwin (1898–1937)	*Porgy and Bess* *Rhapsody in Blue*
Copland (1900–1990)	*Appalachian Spring* *Billy the Kid* *Rodeo* *El Salón Mexico*
Weill (1900–1950)	*The Threepenny Opera*
Rodrigo (1901–1999)	*Concierto de Aranjuez*
Walton (1902–1983)	*Belshazzar's Feast* *Henry V - film score*
Berkeley (1903–1989)	*Serenade for Strings, Op.12*
Khachaturian (1903–1978)	*Spartacus*
Tippett (1905–1998)	*A Child of Our Time*
Shostakovich (1906–1975)	*Symphony No. 1* *24 Preludes and Fugues, Op. 87* *Symphony No. 7 (Leningrad)*
Messiaen (1908–1992)	*Vingt regards sur l'Enfant-Jésus* *Turangalîla-Symphonie* *Catalogue d'oiseaux*
Barber (1910–1981)	*Adagio for Strings* *Symphony in One Movement, Op. 9* *Overture - The School for Scandal*
Cage (1912–1992)	*Sonata and Interludes* - prepared piano

Britten (1913–1976)	*Sea Interludes (Peter Grimes)*
	The Young Person's Guide to the Orchestra
	War Requiem
Lutoslawski (1913–1994)	*Variations on a Theme by Paganini*
	Cello Concerto
	Symphony No. 3
Ginastera (1916–1983)	*Estancia*
	Harp Concerto
Bernstein (1918–1990)	*West Side Story*
	Chichester Psalms
Ligeti (b. 1923)	*Atmosphères*
	Lux aeterna
Berio (b. 1925)	*Sequenzas*
Boulez (b. 1925)	*Le Marteau sans Maître*
	Pli selon pli
Henze (b. 1926)	*El Cimarrón*
	Royal Winter Music (for guitar)
Stockhausen (b. 1928)	*Kontakte*
	Kontra-Punkte
Williamson (b. 1931)	*Our Man in Havana*
Górecki (b. 1933)	*Symphony No. 3*
Penderecki (b. 1933)	*Symphony No. 5*
Birtwistle (b. 1934)	*Punch and Judy* (opera)
	Gawain (opera)
Maxwell Davies (b. 1934)	*Eight Songs for a Mad King*
Pärt (b. 1935)	*Symphony No. 2*
Reich (b. 1936)	*Electric Counterpoint*
	Drumming

Glass (b. 1937)	*Music in Twelve Parts*
	Violin Concerto
Tavener (b. 1944)	*Hymn to the Mother of God*
Adams (b. 1947)	*Short Ride in a Fast Machine*

Suggested further reading

General Music Books

Abraham, Gerald. *The Concise Oxford History of Music,* Oxford University Press and Readers Union, 1979.

Bernstein, Leonard. *The Joy of Music,* London: White Lion Press/New York: Simon and Schuster, 1971.

Cooper, Martin, ed. *The New Oxford History of Music: The Modern Age 1890-1960,* Oxford University Press, 1974.

Hopkins, Antony. *Understanding Music,* London: J.M. Dent, 1979.

Karolyi, Otto. *Introducing Music,* Harmondsworth: Penguin, 1965.

Kendall, Alan. *The Chronicle of Classical Music,* London: Thames and Hudson, 1994.

Mellers, Wilfrid. *Music in a New Found Land: Themes and Developments in the History of American Music,* London: Faber and Faber, 1987.

Raeburn, Michael. *The Chronicle of Opera,* London: Thames and Hudson, 1998.

Sadie, Stanley, ed. with Latham, Alison. *The Cambridge Music Guide,* Cambridge University Press, 1985.

Sadie, Stanley; Tyrrell, John, eds. *New Grove Dictionary of Music and Musicians,* 2nd Edition, Vols 1-29, London: Macmillan, 2001.

Slonimsky, Nicolas. *Baker's Biographical Dictionary of Musicians,* 7th edition, Oxford University Press, 1984.

Books on 20th Century Music

Brindle, Reginald Smith. *The New Music: The Avant-Garde since 1945,* Oxford University Press, 1975.

------------------------------ *Musical Composition,* Oxford University Press,1986.

Ewen, David, ed. *The World of Twentieth Century Music,* 2nd edition, rev. Stephen J. Pettitt, London: Robert Hale, 1991.

Griffiths, Paul. *Modern Music: A Concise History from Debussy to Boulez,* London: Thames & Hudson, 1992.

------------------ *Modern Music and After: Directions since 1945,* Oxford University Press, 1995.

------------------*The Thames and Hudson Dictionary of 20th-Century Music,* London: Thames and Hudson, 1996.

Karolyi, Otto. *Modern American Music: From Charles Ives to the Minimalists,* London: Cygnus Arts/Madison and Teaneck: Fairleigh Dickinson University Press, 1996.

Mertens, Wim. *American Minimal Music,* trans. J. Hautekiet, London: Kahn & Averill, 1983.

Morgan, Robert P. *Twentieth-Century Music,* New York/London: W.W. Norton, 1991.

Morris, Mark. *A Guide to 20th-Century Composers,* London: Methuen, 1996.

Raeburn, Michael; Kendall, Alan. *Heritage of Music, Vol. IV: Music in the Twentieth Century,* Oxford University Press, 1989.

Whittall, Arnold. *Musical Composition in the Twentieth Century,* Oxford University Press, 1999.

Biographical Studies of Composers

Armero, Gonzalo; Persia, Jorge de, eds. *Manuel de Falla: his Life & Works,* London: Omnibus, 1999.

Béhague, Gerard. *Heitor Villa-Lobos: The Search for Brazil's Musical Soul,* University of Texas at Austin, Institute of Latin American Studies, 1994.

Carpenter, Humphrey. *Benjamin Britten: A Biography,* London: Faber and Faber, 1992.

Cooper, Barry. *Beethoven,* The Master Musicians, Oxford University Press, 2000.

Griffiths, Paul. *György Ligeti,* 2nd edition, London: Robson Books, 1997.

Gutman, Robert W. *Mozart, A Cultural Biography,* London: Secker & Warburg, 2000.

Kennedy, Michael. *Portrait of Elgar,* Oxford University Press, 3rd edition, 1987.

Kinderman, William. *Beethoven,* Oxford University Press, 1995.

Lockspeiser, Edward. *Debussy,* London: J.M. Dent, revised edition 1980.

MacDonald, Malcolm. *Schoenberg,* London: J.M. Dent, 1976.

Milne, Hamish. *Bartók - His Life and Times,* Tunbridge Wells: Midas Books/New York: Hippocrene Books, 1982.

Nichols, Roger. *Messiaen,* Oxford University Press, 1986.

------------------ *Debussy Remembered,* London: Faber and Faber, 1992.

Norris, Geoffrey. *Rachmaninoff,* New York: Schirmer, 1994.

Peyser, Joan. *Leonard Bernstein,* London: Bantam, 1987.

Rae, Charles Bodman. *The Music of Lutoslawski,* London: Faber and Faber, 1994.

Robinson, Harlow. *Sergei Prokofiev, A Biography,* London: Robert Hale, 1987.

Siepmann, Jeremy. *Chopin, The Reluctant Romantic,* London: Victor Gollancz, 1995.

Solomon, Maynard. *Mozart, A Life,* London: Pimlico, 1995.

Swafford, Jan. *Johannes Brahms: A Biography,* New York: Alfred A. Knopf, 1997.

Wolff, Christoph. *Johann Sebastian Bach: The Learned Musician,* Oxford University Press, 2000.

Writings by Composers

Boulez, Pierre. *Orientations: Collected Writings,* ed. Jean-Jacques Nattiez, trans. Martin Cooper, London/Boston: Faber and Faber, 1986.

Cage, John. *Silence: Lectures and Writings,* London: Marion Boyars, reprinted 1999.
John Cage:Writer, ed. Richard Kostelanetz, New York: Cooper Square Press, 1993.

Copland, Aaron. *What to Listen for in Music,* New York: McGraw-Hill/Mentor, 1957.
Music and Imagination, Harvard University Press, new edition 1972.

Debussy, Claude, collected by François Lesure. *Debussy on Music,* ed. and trans. Richard Langham Smith, London: Secker & Warburg, 1977.

Henze, Hans Werner. *Bohemian Fifths, An Autobiography,* trans. Stewart Spencer, London: Faber and Faber, 1998.

Messiaen, Olivier. *Olivier Messiaen, Music and Color: Conversations with Claude Samuel,* ed. Claude Samuel, trans. E. Thomas Glasow, Portland, Oregon: Amadeus Press, 1994.

Ravel, Maurice. *A Ravel Reader: Correspondence, Articles, Interviews,* ed. Arbie Orenstein, New York: Columbia University Press, 1990.

Stockhausen, Karlheinz. *Stockhausen on Music,* Lectures and Interviews compiled by Robert Maconie, London/New York: Marion Boyars, 1989.

Acknowledgements

Grateful acknowledgement is due to the following for the use of copyright material or for providing specific and invaluable sources of information. (The editor apologizes for any inadvertent omissions from these acknowledgements and any such errors will be corrected in future editions.)

W. Austin (Dent): Pierre Boulez, Jean-Jacques Nattiez, Martin Cooper (Faber and Faber): Reginald Smith Brindle (Oxford University Press): David Ewen (Robert Hale): Paul Griffiths (Thames and Hudson): Otto Karolyi (Cygnus Arts/Fairleigh Dickinson University Press): Wilfrid Mellers (Faber and Faber): Joan Peyser (Bantam Press): Harlow Robinson (Robert Hale): Claude Samuel (Amadeus Press): Mya Tannenbaum (Oxford University Press): Michael Tilson Thomas (Sony): David Urman, J.M. Thomson (Marion Boyars).

Photocredits:

Peter Burr, p. 8: Northamptonshire Newspapers Ltd, p. 30: Royal Library, Turin, p. 32: Edizioni Bèrben, p. 33:Trustees of the British Museum, London, p. 54: Paul Wilson, p. 84: Stadtarchiv Augsburg, p. 101: Schlossmuseum, Weimar, p. 107: EMI/HMV, p. 127, p. 149: Sony, John Herrick Jackson Music Library, Yale University, p. 143: Deutsche Grammophon, p. 162.

Index

A

Absolute music, 65
Aeolian mode, 20
Aerophones, 29
Aficionado, 40
African music, 8
Agnus Dei, 47
Alap, 40
Albéniz, Isaac, 118
Aleatoric music, 156
Alegrías, 40
Allemande, 60-61
Alpine horn, 30
Answer, 72, 73
Arabic lute, 15, 29
Arabic music, 8, 17, 26
Arias, 53
Arnold, Malcolm, 158
Atonality, 21, 113, 129, 131, 164
Auer, Leopold, 97

B

Bach, C. P. E., 75, 76, 77, 78, 86
Bach, J. C., 86
Bach, J. S., 27, 35, 47, 49, 50, 57,
    58, 59, 60, 62, 68, 70, 75, 78,
    92, 94, 95, 116, 137
Background music, 121
Bagpipe, 29, 30, 62
Balalaika, 29
Ballad opera, 139
Ballade, 106
Ballet, 55, 126, 139, 147, 151, 172
Ballroom, 54, 57
Bamboo pipes, 25
Banjo, 30
Barber, Samuel, 147, 148, 149, 151

Baroque style, 30
Barraqué, Jean, 164
Bartók, Béla, 136, 137, 138, 150,
    158, 160, 163, 168
Bass, 68
Bass guitar, 123
Bassoon, 94
Bax, Arnold, 158
Bebop, 68, 122
Beethoven, Ludwig van, 35, 41, 47, 64,
    70, 78, 80, 90, 91, 92, 96, 99,
    102, 104, 108, 109, 116, 125, 167
Bells, 29
Benedictus, 47
Bennett, Richard Rodney, 158, 165
Berg, Alban, 128, 133, 141
Berio, Luciano, 164
Berkeley, Lennox, 158
Berlioz, Hector, 109, 110, 167
Bernstein, Leonard, 162, 163
Binary, 43, 44, 45, 60, 77
Birtwistle, Harrison, 158, 165
Bizet, Georges, 55
Bliss, Arthur, 158
Blues, 51, 147
Borodin, Alexander, 118
Boulanger, Nadia, 147
Boulez, Pierre, 164, 165, 166, 167
Bourrée, 60, 61, 62
Brahms, Johannes, 68, 70, 92, 96, 97,
    116, 117
Bridge, Frank, 158
Bridge passage, 82, 83
Brindle, Reginald Smith, 163, 164
Britten, Benjamin, 50, 67, 158
Broadway, 162, 172
Brodsky, Adolf, 97
Brouwer, Leo, 165

Bruckner, Anton, 92
Budapest Conservatory, 168
Buffalo Festival of the Arts, 169
Burlesca, 60
BWV number, 63
Byron, Lord George Gordon, 110

C

Cadenza, 98
Cage, John, 128, 155, 156, 157, 161
Cantata, 68, 75
Cantus planus, 18
Capriccio, 117
Caprice, 60
Cardew, Cornelius, 165
Carols, 49
Casella, Alfredo, 150, 151
Cello, 29, 58, 78, 87, 94
Chaconne, 68
Chamber music, 139, 144, 149, 172
Chance operations, 156
Children's games, 64
Chopin, Frédéric, 35, 96, 105, 106,
    107, 108, 129
Choral music, 19, 26, 27, 144,
    158, 162
Chord clusters, 144, 168
Chordal sequences, 28
Chordophones, 29
Chôros, 136
Chromaticism, 107, 113, 129, 131
Church modes, 125, 137
Cittern, 30
Clarinet, 29, 96
Classical Era, 78, 79, 80, 81
Classicism, 103
Clementine, 43
Coda, 73, 83
Concert hall, 84, 85
Concertino, 94

Concerto, 77, 94, 95, 96, 97, 98,
    99, 103, 116, 135,
    138, 139, 146, 158, 172
Concerto grosso, 94
Concrete music, 169
Conductor, 85
Congressional Gold Medal, 148
Continuo, 94
Contrapunctus, 26
Contrapuntal, 26, 28
Controlled aleatoricism, 161
Copland, Aaron, 147-148, 162
Corelli, Arcangelo, 86, 94
Counterpoint, 14, 25, 26, 27, 28
Countersubject, 72
Courante, 60, 61
Cowell, Henry, 144, 155
Credo, 47
Crumb, George, 165
Crumhorns, 30
Cubists, 127
Cymbals, 29

D

Dalí, Salvador, 134
Dallapiccola, Luigi, 151
Dance, 54, 55, 56, 57, 60, 61,
    62, 63, 64, 97
Dance band, 122
Davies, Peter Maxwell, 158, 165
Debussy, Claude, 123, 124, 125, 127,
    129, 134, 136, 160, 167
Degrees of the scale, 22
Delius, Frederick, 158
Deutsch, Otto Erich, 63
Development, 77, 82, 99
Diatonic scale, 137
Didgeridoo, 30
Dies Irae, 47
Dissonance, 144, 150
Dominant, 22, 72, 76, 82
Double bass, 87

Doubles, 60
Dowland, John, 67, 104
Drone bass, 62
Drum, 29
Duration, 32
Dvořák, Antonín, 47, 117, 118

E

Early music, 30, 34
Ecclesiastical music, 27
Electronic feedback, 12
Electronic music, 157, 168, 169
Elgar, Edward, 48, 67, 92, 158
Eliot, T. S., 123
Ellington, Duke, 36
Episodes, 64, 73
Études, 106
Ewen, David, 165
Exposition, 72, 73, 81, 82, 98

F

Falla, Manuel de, 134, 135
Fandango, 40
Fantasia, 60, 76
Fauré, Gabriel, 47, 125, 150
Film music, 148, 157, 161, 169, 171, 173
First movement, 80, 81, 82
First Subject, 81, 82, 83
Flamenco, 8, 40, 134
Flute, 29, 94, 96
Folk dances, 139
Folk song, 26, 42, 51, 134, 137, 138,
    158, 161·
Form, 38, 39, 40, 41, 42, 43, 44,
    45, 164
Formalism, 142, 161
Foss, Lukas, 164
Fourth movement, 80
Franck, César, 70
French overture, 86
Fricker, Peter Racine, 158

Froberger, Johann Jacob, 59
Fugue, 70-74
Fürnberg, Baron Joseph von, 78
Furniture music, 128

G

Gavotte, 60, 61, 62
Gebrauchsmusik, 141
Gerhard, Roberto, 135
German opera, 112, 113, 114
German romanticism, 112, 113
Gershwin, George, 144, 146, 162
Gigue, 60, 62
Glasow, E. Thomas, 153, 154
Glass, Philip, 171
Glockenspiel, 29
Gloria, 47
Goehr, Alexander, 165
Goethe, Johann von, 111
Górecki, Henryk, 165
Gospel songs, 49
Gossec, François-Joseph, 86
Graphic notation, 156
Greek modes, 137
Greek Orthodox Church, 159
Gregorian chant, 18, 25, 49
Grieg, Edvard, 117, 118
Griffiths, Paul, 126
Ground bass, 68
Guitar, 12, 15, 29, 123, 137, 167

H

Handel, George Frideric,
    48, 53, 70, 94
Harmonic minor scale, 20
Harmonica, 30
Harmony, 14, 21, 25, 28, 144, 156, 164
Harp, 29, 96
Harpsichord, 30
Harris, Roy, 144
Haydn, Joseph, 48, 63, 64, 78, 80,
    88, 89, 90, 95, 96, 108

Henderson, W. J., 145
Henze, Hans Werner, 164
Hindemith, Paul, 70, 141, 151, 163
Hoboken, Anthony van, 63
Horn, 96
Hungarian folk music, 137, 138
Hymns, 49

I

I Ching, 156
Idée fixe, 109
Idiophones, 29
Impressionism, 123, 127, 158
Impromptu, 106
Improvisation, 9, 35, 36, 68, 144
Indeterminacy, 156, 170
Indian music, 8, 14, 26, 39,
    40, 153, 159
Indy, Vincent d', 128
Instrumental music, 57
Intermezzo, 117
Ionian mode, 19
Ireland, John, 158
Italian opera, 111, 115
Italian overture, 86
Ives, Charles, 143–144

J

Janacek, Leos, 118
Jazz, 36, 42, 43, 68, 122, 143,
    146, 147, 172
Jhala, 40
Jig, 62
Jor, 40
Joyce, James, 123

K

Karolyi, Otto, 149
Kettledrum, 89
Key, 21
Keyboard, 58, 123

Keyboard concertos, 94, 96
Keynote, 21
Kirkpatrick, Ralph, 63
Köchel, Ludwig von, 63
Kodály, Zoltán, 136-139
Koto, 30
Kubrick, Stanley, 169
Kyrie eleison, 47

L

Leading note, 22, 23
Leitmotiv, 109, 113
Libretto, 51
Ligeti, György, 164, 168, 169
Liszt, Franz, 35, 96, 105, 107,
    108, 111, 117
Loure, 60
Lully, Jean-Baptiste, 86
Lute, 29, 30, 58
Lutoslawski, Witold, 160-162
Lyric drama, 135

M

Maderna, Bruno, 164
Mahler, Gustav, 92, 129
Malagueña, 40
Malipiero, Gian Francesco, 150
Mallarmé, Stéphane, 167
Mandolin, 94
Marching songs, 26
Mascagni, Pietro, 115
Mass, 47
Mass for the Dead, 47
Mazurka, 61, 106
Mediant, 22, 23
Medieval modes, 159
Melody, 25, 26, 42, 43, 64, 65, 66,
    67, 71, 76, 82, 129, 156, 164
Membranophones, 29
Mendelssohn, Felix, 48, 49, 70, 92,
    110, 111

Menotti, Gian Carlo, 151
Messiaen, Olivier, 152, 153, 154, 155, 165, 169
Metronomes, 169
Microtones, 16
Middle Ages, 11, 16, 30
Middle eight, 43
Middle section, 82
Milhaud, Darius, 147
Minimalism, 156, 171
Minuet, 60, 61, 62, 74, 80, 85, 97
Miró, Joán, 134
Modes, 16, 19, 20, 125, 137
Modes of limited transpositions, 154
Modulation, 23, 82
Mompou, Federico, 135
Monteverdi, Claudio, 53, 150
Mozart, Wolfgang Amadeus, 35, 47, 63, 64, 70, 78, 89, 90, 95, 96, 98, 101, 108
Musette, 62
Music and movement, 54
Music and words, 46, 51
Musical form, 38-43, 66, 67
Musical instruments, 29, 30, 31
Musicals, 51, 172
Musique concrète, 169
Musique d'ameublement, 128
Mussorgsky, Modest, 118

N

Nationalism, 107, 112, 117, 118
NBC Symphony Orchestra, 148
Neoclassicism, 140, 161
Nocturne, 106
Nono, Luigi, 164
Notation, 9, 25, 32, 33, 34, 35, 36, 37
Note row, 132

O

Oboe, 94

Octave, 15, 16, 19, 105, 125
Opera, 36, 41, 51, 52, 53, 86, 101, 102, 111, 112, 113, 114, 115, 133, 149, 151, 158, 169, 172
Oratorio, 48, 49, 158
Orchestra, 11, 31, 32, 36, 41, 49, 58, 84, 85, 86, 87, 88, 89, 97, 98, 99, 110, 144, 170
Orchestration, 126, 139
Oriental music, 8, 17, 26
Oscillators, 156
Overture, 60, 86, 110, 111

P

Paganini, Nicolò, 96, 107
Palestrina, Giovanni Perluigi da, 27, 47
Paris Conservatoire, 165
Partita, 58
Passacaglia, 68
Passepied, 60
Passion, 48, 49
Penderecki, Krzystof, 165
Pentatonic, 125, 137
Percussion, 26, 156, 167, 170
Petrassi, Goffredo, 151
Peyser, Joan, 163
Phrasing, 32
Pianoforte, 11, 105, 106, 107, 108, 117, 118, 125, 127, 128, 137, 139, 144, 149, 171
Picasso, Pablo, 123, 134, 139, 140
Pipes of Pan, 30
Piston, Walter, 144
Plainsong, 18, 20
Pointillism, 169
Polonaise, 106
Polyphony, 26, 27
Polyrhythms, 144
Pope Gregory I, 18
Pre-recorded magnetic tape, 156
Prelude, 60, 76, 106

Prepared piano, 156
Program music, 104, 106
Prokofiev, Sergei, 142, 147
Psalms, 18
Puccini, Giacomo, 115, 150

R

Rachmaninoff, Sergei, 92, 96, 118
Ragas, 39, 40
Rameau, Jean-Philippe, 104
Ravel, Maurice, 125, 126, 134, 136
Recapitulation, 82, 99
Recitative, 53
Recorder, 30, 32, 94
Recording technology, 120
Reich, Steve, 171
Relative major, 24
Relative minor, 24
Repetition, 42
Requiem, 47
Rhapsody, 117
Riley, Terry, 171
Rimsky-Korsakov, Nikolai, 118
Ripieno, 94
Rock music, 122, 123, 143, 157, 172
Rodrigo, Joaquín, 99, 135
Romanian folk music, 137
Romanticism, 103, 104, 105, 108, 109,
    112, 118, 133, 140
Rondeau, rondo, 60, 63, 64, 74
Rossini, Gioachino, 111
Roussel, Albert, 128
Rubato, 107
Ruggles, Carl, 144
Russian romanticism, 118
Ryom, Peter, 63

S

Sackbut, 30
Sacred music, 46, 47, 48, 49, 50,
    51, 172

Salomon symphonies, 89
Sammartini, Giovanni Batista, 86
Sanctus, 47
Sarabande, 60, 61
Sarod, 39
Satie, Erik, 127, 128, 135
Saxophone, 121
Scales, 14, 15, 16, 17, 20, 21, 22, 23
Scarlatti, Domenico, 63, 75, 76
Schaeffer, Peter, 169
Scherzo, 60, 80, 85, 97, 106
Schiller, Friedrich, 91
Schmieder, Wolfgang, 63
Schoenberg, Arnold, 128-133, 134,
    135, 137, 138, 139, 141, 150,
    152, 155, 163, 164, 165, 168
Schola Cantorum, Paris, 128
Schubert, Franz, 42, 63, 77, 92, 108
Schumann, Robert, 92, 105, 108
Scottish reels, 42
Scriabin, Alexander, 129
Second movement, 80
Second Subject, 82, 83
Second World War, 158, 163
Serialism, 132, 144, 156, 163, 164,
    165, 166, 168, 170
Sessions, Roger, 144
Shakespeare, William, 30, 110
Shofar, 30
Shostakovich, Dmitri, 70, 92, 142
Shrutis, 16
Sibelius, Jean, 92, 118
Sinfonia concertante, 96
Sitar, 15, 29, 39
Smetana, Bedrich, 118
Soleares, 40
Soli, 94
Soloist, 94, 96, 97, 98, 99
Sonata, 74, 75, 78, 80, 81, 82,
    86, 87, 88, 103, 108, 116
Sonata form, 78, 81, 108
Sonata rondo form, 64

Spanish music, 40, 133-135
Stamitz, Johann, 86
Stockhausen, Karlheinz, 164, 169, 170, 171
Strauss, Richard, 129
Stravinsky, Igor, 49, 136, 139, 140, 141, 147, 150, 154, 162, 163
Streets of Laredo, 43, 44
Stretto, 73
String quartet, 77, 79, 80, 81, 88, 133, 138, 144, 148, 149, 171
Stringed gourd, 25
Subdominant, 22, 23
Subject, 72, 73
Submediant, 22, 23
Suite, 42, 58, 59, 60, 61, 62, 66, 76, 77, 125, 139
Supertonic, 22, 23
Symmetrical permutations, 155
Symphonic poem, 111
Symphony, 31, 36, 41, 42, 77, 80, 81, 84, 85, 86, 87, 88, 89, 90, 91, 92, 96, 103, 109, 111, 116, 118, 139, 144, 158, 161, 162, 172
Symphony orchestra, 84
Synthesizer, 12

T

Takemitsu, Toru, 165
Tal, 40
Tannenbaum, Mya, 169
Tape recorders, 12, 157, 169
Tavener, John, 159
Tchaikovsky, Piotr Ilyich, 92, 97, 117, 118
Telemann, Georg Philipp, 94
Ternary, 43, 44, 45, 64, 43
Theme and variations, 65, 66, 67
Third movement, 80, 99
Thomas, Michael Tilson, 144
Thomson, Virgil, 144
Time-space projects, 171

Tippett, Michael, 158
Tonality, 20-24
Tone poem, 111
Tone row, 132, 139
Tonic, 21, 22, 23, 76, 81, 82, 83
Tonreihe, 132
Torroba, Federico Moreno, 135
Toscanini, Arturo, 148
Total serialism, 165, 166
Triangle, 29
Trio, 80, 85, 97
Trombone, 30
Trumpet, 29, 94
Turina, Joaquín, 135
Twelve-tone, 128, 132, 133, 137, 151, 165
Twelve-tone opera, 151

V

Varèse, Edgard, 144, 145
Variations, 60, 65, 66, 67, 68, 74, 116, 117, 146
Vaughan Williams, Ralph, 158
Verdi, Giuseppe, 47, 114, 115, 118, 150
Verismo, 115
Villa-Lobos, Heitor, 136, 137
Viol, 30, 86, 87
Viola, 78, 87, 96
Violin, 15, 58, 78, 87, 96, 121
Violin concerto, 94, 96, 97
Vivaldi, Antonio, 63, 94, 104, 150
Voice, 13, 25, 33

W

Wagenseil, Georg Christoph, 86
Wagner, Richard, 109, 112, 113, 114, 129, 167
Walton, William, 158
Waltz, 106
Weber, Carl Maria von, 112
Webern, Anton, 128, 133, 134, 140, 141, 164, 168

When the Saints Go Marching In, 43
Whistle, 29
Whole tone scale, 125
Williamson, Malcolm, 158
Work songs, 26

X

Xenakis, Iannis, 164
Xylophone, 29

Y

Young, La Monte, 171

Z

Zen, 156